FILM FOCUS

Ronald Gottesman and Harry M. Geduld
General Editors

THE FILM FOCUS SERIES PRESENTS THE BEST THAT HAS BEEN
WRITTEN ABOUT THE ART OF FILM AND THE MEN WHO CREATED
IT. COMBINING CRITICISM WITH HISTORY, BIOGRAPHY, AND ANAL-
YSIS OF TECHNIQUE, THE VOLUMES IN THE SERIES EXPLORE THE
MANY DIMENSIONS OF THE FILM MEDIUM AND ITS IMPACT ON
MODERN SOCIETY.

HARRY M. GEDULD *is Professor of English and Comparative
Literature at Indiana University, where he helped to establish a flourishing film study program. A member of the Society for Cinema Studies, he has written several books and
numerous movie reviews for American publications.*

FOCUS ON

D. W. GRIFFITH

edited by
HARRY M. GEDULD

A SPECTRUM BOOK

Prentice-Hall, Inc.
Englewood Cliffs, N.J.

Grateful acknowledgment is made to Doug Moore for his encouragement and for the loan of many Biograph films, and to David Thaxton for providing a copy of the NAACP pamphlet on *The Birth of a Nation* and for supplying information about some basic source material.

Illustrations are reprinted from *Lillian Gish: The Movies, Mr. Griffith and Me* by Lillian Gish with Ann Pinchot (Englewood Cliffs, N.J.: Prentice-Hall, Inc., 1969). Copyright © 1969 by Lillian Gish and Ann Pinchot. All rights reserved. Reprinted by permission of Lucy Kroll Agency and The Museum of Modern Art/Film Stills Archive.

C–13-365205-X
P–13-365197–5
Library of Congress Catalog Card Number 78–153435

Printed in the United States of America.

Current printing (last number):
10 9 8 7 6 5 4 3 2

Prentice-Hall International, Inc. (*London*)
Prentice-Hall of Australia, Pty. Ltd. (*Sydney*)
Prentice-Hall of Canada, Ltd. (*Toronto*)
Prentice-Hall of India Private Limited (*New Delhi*)
Prentice-Hall of Japan, Inc. (*Tokyo*)

for Marcus again
and also for
Dollie, Judith, Elsie, and Flora,
the Little Dear One, the Mountain Girl,
and Lucy

CONTENTS

ESSAYS

"The task I'm trying to achieve is above all to make you see."
—D. W. GRIFFITH

Introduction
by HARRY M. GEDULD

Film art is the only art the development of which men now living have witnessed from the very beginning; and this development is all the more interesting as it took place under conditions contrary to precedent. It was not an artistic urge that gave rise to the discovery and gradual perfection of a new technique; it was a technical invention that gave rise to the discovery and gradual perfection of a new art.[1]

In his admirable book, *Mechanization Takes Command,* Siegfried Giedion shows how the analysis and synthesis of movement are basic to the processes of mechanization.[2] But the developments that proceeded from the earliest graphic representation of movement (by Nicolas Oresme in the fourteenth century) to Frank B. Gilbreth's time-and-motion studies in the twentieth century resulted not only in the conveyor belt and mass production, but also in the evolution of the motion picture. In short, the ideas and principles that produced mechanization also produced, contemporaneously, a new medium of expression for the mechanized age. And it was D. W. Griffith, above all, who was responsible for shaping that new medium of expression, the motion picture, into an art form.

It is given to few men to create a new art—and on the face of it Griffith seems to have had a most unlikely preparation for such a distinction. Son of a Confederate colonel; scion of the Old South and its mystique; sometime itinerant actor, schooled in the well-made play and late nineteenth-century melodrama; a failed dramatist who was forced through economic straits and to his humiliation to seek out em-

---

[1] Erwin Panofsky, "Style and Medium in the Motion Pictures," *Transition* (Paris), no. 26 (Winter, 1937), p. 121.

[2] Siegfried Giedion, *Mechanization Takes Command* (New York: Norton, 1969). See especially pp. 14–31, 110–15.

1

ployment in the "primitive" American film industry and who was later drafted reluctantly into the job of film directing without any knowledge of either the motion picture camera or of what the job of directing involved—such was the background of the first great motion-picture director—and perhaps the greatest. Yet in the brief span of eight years, from 1908 through 1915, this unpromising and reluctant film-maker directed approximately 500 films (mostly one- and two-reelers) and transformed the crude flickering entertainment of the nickelodeons into the century's most powerful medium for propaganda—and into a new art whose commercial success threatened the very existence of the "legitimate theater."

This book is a collection of biographical and commentative writings by and about D. W. Griffith. In it the reader will find accounts of Griffith's early life, his entrance into the film industry, and his work for the Biograph Company. But the main focus of the book is, of course, upon Griffith's mature creative work, his artistic and technical achievements, and his reputation. Included are analyses and evaluations of many of his films, a survey of their technical and narrative developments, and examples of many of the charges brought against his most controversial film, *The Birth of a Nation.* The volume also contains a generous selection of Griffith's own writings, most of which have not appeared in print since their original appearance in periodical publications over forty years ago.

The opening biographical section contains a little-known autobiographical statement by Griffith, tantalizing for what it suggests about the writer's struggles—both material and psychological. The dedicated student will doubtless wish to augment this brief statement by consulting Griffith's unpublished memoir and notes for a projected autobiography (preserved in the Museum of Modern Art Film Library, New York City)—a work that could not, unfortunately, be included in the present volume.

The other piece in the biographical section is excerpted from *When the Movies Were Young* (1925) by Linda Arvidson, the first Mrs. D. W. Griffith. This is a book that has become primary source material for all who are seriously interested in Griffith's career up through the making of *The Birth of a Nation* (1915). Mrs. Griffith's book continues the story begun in Griffith's brief autobiographical statement. After a brief spell as an actor for the Edison Company, under Edwin S. Porter's direction, Griffith, in 1908, sought out employment with the Biograph Company (11 East Fourteenth Street, New York City), at first as an actor, then later, reluctantly, as a movie director. In the five years he was to remain with Biograph, Griffith was to develop the techniques that shaped his major films and the entire future of motion-picture art. The excerpt from Mrs. Griffith's book recounts the circumstances in which Griffith came to direct his first movie, *The Adventures of Dollie* (1908).

There follows an interview with the director, originally published three days before the première of *The Birth of a Nation*. It provides us with a vivid impression of the man on the eve of his greatest commercial and (arguably) his greatest artistic triumph, as well as authoritative comments on the film and a few provocative expressions of hope and prophecy for the motion picture. Other interviews with Griffith are listed in the bibliography or given—in excerpt—later in the anthology.

One section of this book is devoted to Griffith's own observations, mainly on film and related subjects. This is the only selection of Griffith's writings published to date, and though they do not reveal him as a great theoretician—like Eisenstein—they will, nevertheless be of unique interest to all who are concerned with the work of the American film master. Many of the items published here originally appeared in periodicals that are now virtually inaccessible to the majority of readers.

In the bibliography will be found additional items by Griffith which could not be included in the present selection.[3] Some of the items that *have* been included are published in their entirety; others have been divested of the original editorializing that is often superficial; while a few brief excerpts have been taken from articles or interviews which were considered too ephemeral to bear republishing as a whole.

This selection of Griffith's own writings is arranged chronologically in order of original publication—which serves sometimes to indicate the development of Griffith's ideas on a particular topic. Of particular importance to film scholars are: "Working for the Biograph Company" (in which Griffith outlines the original purposes of some of his technical innovations); "How I made *The Birth of a Nation*"; the excerpt from Griffith's pamphlet, *The Rise and Fall of Free Speech in America* (a polemic originally intended as a counterblast to the furor over *The Birth of a Nation* and as preparation for the release of the film, *Intolerance*, 1916); "Concerning *Intolerance*: Interview with Griffith"; and the observations on film acting in such pieces as "What I Demand of Movie Stars" and "Youth, the Spirit of the Movies." Several items included are strongly flavored with prophecy—and here the reader is likely to be both impressed with Griffith's prescience and amused or surprised at his occasional "shortsightedness."

The reader who checks sources will note that several items included in the selection of Griffith's writings have been taken from a serialized

---

[3] Regrettably, it was impossible to include excerpts from Griffith's two plays: *The Fool and the Girl* (in manuscript in the Rare Books division of the Library of Congress) and *War* (in manuscript in the Museum of Modern Art Film Library, New York).

biography of Griffith by Henry Stephen Gordon, first published in *Photoplay* (June–November 1916). This biography is based on long interviews with Griffith which have become, like Linda Arvidson's book, primary source material. In their original form, however, these interviews are padded with observations by Gordon that usually leave much to be desired as commentary. Thus, in including the material here, most of Gordon's remarks have been stripped away, leaving, for the most part, the text of Griffith's statements to his interviewer-biographer.

Much of the remainder of the book consists of a selection of the most important commentary and criticism on Griffith. Regrettably, here the editor has had to omit one piece of major critical significance. This is Sergei M. Eisenstein's long essay, "Dickens, Griffith, and the Film Today," [4] which cannot be recommended too highly. No student of Griffith's—or Eisenstein's—work can afford to ignore that essay, which is included in Eisenstein's book, *Film Form*.

The pieces that *have* been included have been arranged generally in relation to their application to the chronology of Griffith's work. Thus, we begin the essay section with an article by A. Nicholas Vardac that discusses technical innovations in the Biograph films, and, in particular, their demonstration of Griffith's "heightening [of] the realism of the camera, of acting, and of . . . production," his movement "toward a refinement and articulation" of melodramatic cinematic syntax, and his "enlargement of the pictorial and productional conception of the film through the addition of spectacle." Vardac's commentary has been taken from his book, *Stage to Screen* (1949), in which he considers how early cinema—in particular Griffith's films (the creations of a one-time stage actor)—inherited the melodramatic traditions of nineteenth-century theatre; this topic is dealt with most perceptibly towards the end of the excerpted piece.

There follows a selection of commentary on *The Birth of a Nation* (1915). First, another piece by Mrs. Griffith—a factual account of how Griffith came to make the film. Then a later excerpt from Vardac's book, discussing concisely but significantly the qualities that made the picture a success and a major influence on the art of film: in particular, its dynamic editorial techniques, its simulation of authenticity, and its skillful fusion of melodrama and spectacle. British critic Paul O'Dell provides an additional perspective on the technical achievements of *The Birth of a Nation*, and the concentration on this particular film concludes with a selection of adverse critical and polemical observations culled from an NAACP pamphlet issued at the time of the film's

[4] Completed in 1944. See Sergei M. Eisenstein, *Film Form*, edited and translated by Jay Leyda (New York: Harcourt, Brace & World, Inc., 1949), pp. 195–255.

première in Boston, 1915, and exemplifying the reactions that developed into riots in some cities where the film was shown.

Commentary on *Intolerance* (1916) is represented by Lewis Jacobs' acute analysis from his *The Rise of the American Film*.

The articles that follow are both significant "by-products" of the second retrospective of films by D. W. Griffith, presented at the Museum of Modern Art, New York City, April 25 through July 31, 1965. At this retrospective, some forty-two of Griffith's films were shown, representing the entire range of his work from his early Biograph pictures through to his last feature film, *The Struggle* (1931). Two of those who attended this presentation were Dr. Richard J. Meyer and Professor G. Charles Niemeyer. Following the retrospective programs, Dr. Meyer prepared a study of the development of themes and techniques in the forty films he had seen; while Professor Niemeyer undertook an original attempt to rank Griffith's feature films on the basis of their artistic achievement. The work of both scholars appears here—revised, corrected, and updated expressly for this book —providing invaluable complementary surveys of Griffith's *oeuvre*.

The section of commentary and criticism concludes with several pieces that focus on Griffith's personality, his final years of enforced obscurity, his death and enduring reputation. The first of two excerpts from Lillian Gish's *The Movies, Mr. Griffith, and Me* provides an intimate view of Griffith the man—about whom it was "impossible to be neutral. . . . Like all men of great stature, he inspired both admiration and dislike. His secretary Agnes Wiener, who probably knew him as well as anyone did, thought that the reason Mr. Griffith was considered 'odd' and 'lonely' was that he was an intellectual giant among pygmies. . . ." A second excerpt from Miss Gish's book gives us a disturbing glimpse of Griffith at the end of his directorial career. There follows a moving tribute to Griffith by his most eminent "student"—the director and actor Erich von Stroheim. The selection concludes with Jay Leyda's article, "The Art and Death of D. W. Griffith." Inspired by the occasion of Griffith's funeral, Mr. Leyda offers a sensitive and sometimes painfully honest assessment of Griffith's shortcomings and achievements, observing that none of his material conflicts was "as bloody as the conflicts with his own inadequacies. An instinct for beauty clashed with a desperate wish for 'culture' . . ." And within his greatest films, passion and substance were perpetually at war with one another.

Anyone seeking to acquire a full understanding of Griffith's work must prepare to brace himself for the task of becoming familiar with a vast body of films, the majority of which are not easily accessible— and some of which are no longer extant and thus can be known only through reviews and other descriptive accounts. The ramifications of such serious study of Griffith's work would soon be found to extend far beyond the subject-matter of the films themselves. Thus, the Biograph films absorbed many of the traditions and formulas of nineteenth-century American theatre—traditions that must be comprehended if Griffith's selection and treatment of story material and his direction of movie actors are to be understood. But if Griffith had simply transferred theatrical traditions to the screen, his movies would now be of little more than "antiquarian" interest. He was, first and foremost, a master of cinematic technique, as many of the Biograph films reveal—particularly to those students of film who are aware of the extremely limited range of the motion picture before he appeared on the scene. On December 31, 1913, Griffith, in announcing his break with the Biograph Company, published in *The New York Dramatic Mirror* an advertisement specifying the technical discoveries to which he laid claim:

D. W. Griffith
Producer of all great Biograph successes,
revolutionizing Motion Picture drama
and founding the modern technique of the art.

Included in the innovations which he introduced and which are now generally followed by the most advanced producers, are: The large or close-up figures, distant views as represented first in *Ramona,* the "switchback," sustained suspense, the "fade-out," and restraint in expression, raising motion-picture acting to the higher plane which has won for it recognition as a genuine art. . . .

Unfortunately, Griffith cannot be credited with being the *innovator* of most of these techniques. Examination of the films of earlier film-makers—particularly the films that have recently become available from the Library of Congress Paper Print Collection—reveal many of these "innovations" in movies that were made before Griffith set foot inside a movie studio. But Griffith *does* seem to have introduced the switchback (or flashback), in his Biograph film, *The Fatal Hour* (1908) and he was the first to use certain lighting effects in films—though he seems to have taken over those effects from theatre lighting techniques.[5]

Griffith's major technical "innovation" was in using the discoveries of others for intelligent *dramatic* purposes. Thus, while he did not actually "invent" the close-up, for example, he was the first film-maker

[5] Robert Henderson, in his *D. W. Griffith: The Years at Biograph* (New York: Farrar, Straus & Giroux, 1970), pp. 165–77, disposes of many of Griffith's claims to technical innovation.

to make use of it as an integral part of narrative or character development. By discovering and showing how and when to use the techniques that others had originated, he enlarged the scope of the medium beyond the wildest dreams of the motion-picture pioneers who preceded him. How did this come about?

"In the earliest years of its existence," observed Pudovkin, "the film was no more than an interesting invention that made it possible to record movements. . . . The first attempts to relate cinematography to the world of art were naturally bound up with the Theatre. . . . The film remained, as before, but living photography. Art did not enter into the work of him who made it. He only photographed the 'art of the actor.' . . . To sum up in short, the work of the film producer differed in no wise from that of the theatrical producer. . . . But with the grasping of the concept *editing,* the position became basically altered. The real material of film-art proved to be not those actual scenes on which the lens of the camera is directed. . . ." [6] The first step had been taken by Edwin S. Porter, whose films, *The Life of an American Fireman* (1902) and *The Great Train Robbery* (1903), had introduced the method of action continuity into motion-picture narrative. In Porter's two most important films, as Karel Reisz has pointed out, "only the significant parts of the story are selected and joined to form an acceptable, logically developing continuity. Porter had demonstrated that the single shot, recording an incomplete piece of action, is the unit of which films must be constructed and thereby established the basic principle of editing." [7] Griffith's advances over Porter—to whom the movie camera was seldom more than an objective or impartial recorder of the dramatic scene—were essentially (1) to turn the movie camera into an *active* observer, and (2) to demonstrate how, in filming any story, it was the inherent *dramatic ideas* that had to determine the selection, sequence, and timing of the shots (or "incomplete actions") that were filmed, and then assembled in the process of editing. From Griffith's method of editing through "dramatic continuity" all motion-picture narrative techniques have been evolved. Thus, there is no story film, and certainly no masterwork of the cinema that is not directly influenced by the achievements of Griffith during his prolific Biograph period.

However, it is *The Birth of a Nation* and *Intolerance* rather than the Biograph films that generally come to mind first in any consideration of Griffith's work and influence. This is natural enough, since these are the two of his motion pictures most frequently revived and the major works on which his enduring reputation rests. In both films, as

[6] V. I. Pudovkin, *Film Technique,* translated by Ivor Montagu (London: George Newnes, 1933), pp. 51–53, 55.
[7] Karel Reisz, *The Technique of Film Editing* (London: Focal Press, 1966), p. 19.

Pudovkin noted, are combined in an unforgettable manner "the inner dramatic content of the action and a masterly employment of external effort (dynamic tension)." [8]

The importance of *The Birth of a Nation* can hardly be overstated. It is perhaps the most influential and controversial film in the entire history of motion pictures. Some critics—most recently Herman G. Weinberg—have singled it out as "the film that started it all." [9] It was, of course, the dynamic synthesis of all the cinematic techniques developed by Griffith since he had directed his first movie. But far more than that: it was the first film to reveal the vast potentialities of the motion picture as a vehicle for propaganda. It was the first film to be taken seriously as a political statement and it has never failed to be regarded seriously as a "sociological document." Violent controversy, nation-wide demands for federal or state censorship of the motion pictures, and sometimes riots (as in Boston) followed in its wake, so that people who had previously dismissed the movies as nothing more than a crude entertainment suddenly realized that they had become the century's most potent and provocative medium of expression: the mechanized age had produced mass communications, mass entertainment, and also the possibility of mass indoctrination. But some of the consequences were far from ominous or insidious. To many people who had held themselves aloof from the cinema, *The Birth of a Nation* was the film that conferred "respectability" on the medium: President Wilson had seen it at a private showing in the White House, and numerous educationists, historians, and politicians commented publicly upon the "educational" importance of the picture. Moreover, critics had arisen, hailing the motion picture as a new art-form, and *The Birth of a Nation* as its first genuine masterwork.

Neither *The Birth of a Nation* nor *Intolerance* substantiate Rilke's view that works of art are always "products . . . of having-gone-to-the-very-end in an experience, to where man can go no further." To the contrary, both were, in fact, seminal works—motion pictures that threw open for all future film-makers the vast potentialities of the new art form. *The Birth of a Nation,* while it heightened a perversion of history and the dogma of racism to the level of art, also indicated the rich possibilities inherent in applying the techniques of the motion picture to the imaginative interpretation of documentary material.

It was said by Walter Pater that all art constantly aspires towards the condition of music. Through Griffith the art of film achieved this aspiration—or something very close to it—within twenty years after the inception of the motion picture. *Intolerance,* made less than ten years

---

[8] Pudovkin, op. cit., p. 20.

[9] Herman G. Weinberg, *Saint Cinema* (New York: DBS Publications, 1970), p. 16.

after *The Adventures of Dollie,* demonstrated in its pictorial brilliance, in its powerful, rhythmic cutting and in its daring counterpoint of images and narratives that film was capable of producing the visual equivalent of great and complex symphonic music. It was this film, perhaps even more than *The Birth of a Nation,* that justified Griffith's assertion, made in 1914: "The motion picture, although a growth of only a few years, is boundless in its scope and endless in its possibilities. The whole world is its stage, and time without end its limitations."

Chronology

1875   David Wark Griffith born on January 22, 1875, at Crestwood, Kentucky. He was the fourth son of Jacob Wark Griffith, a former Confederate Colonel, and his wife, Mary Perkins Oglesby Griffith.

1895–   DWG undertook a great variety of jobs: elevator boy, bookstore assistant, newspaper reporter for *The Courier-Journal* (Louisville, Ky.), book and journal salesman, hop-picker, ore-puddler, actor in numerous stock company productions. Professional stage name: "Lawrence Griffith."

1906   Married Linda Arvidson, an actress.

1907   DWG's play, *The Fool and the Girl,* produced in Washington and Baltimore.

1908   Employed by the Edison [Film] Company in The Bronx, New York City. Played his first film role in Edwin S. Porter's *Rescued from an Eagle's Nest.* Joined the Biograph Company as film actor; later, reluctantly, became film director. July 14, 1908—release of *The Adventures of Dollie,* the first film directed by DWG.

1914   March 7—release of his four-reel epic film, *Judith of Bethulia,* the last film he directed for the Biograph Company.

1915   Premiere of DWG's film, *The Clansman,* February 8 at Clune's Auditorium, Los Angeles; for the New York premiere, March 3, at the Liberty Theatre, the film's title was changed to *The Birth of a Nation.*

1916   Preview of *Intolerance* at Riverside, California, August 6, 1916; the film premiere in New York occurred September 5, 1916, at the Liberty Theatre.

1917   Visited the Western Front as guest of British Army High Command and the British Government; filmed scenes of the conflict that were afterwards incorporated into *Hearts of the World,* 1918.

1919   Premiere of *Broken Blossoms,* May 13, at the George M. Cohan Theatre, New York.

1920   Premiere of *Way Down East*: previewed in Middletown and Kingston, New York; New York City premiere September 3, at the 44th Street Theatre.

1921   *Orphans of the Storm* opened in Boston, December 28, and in New York at the Apollo Theatre, January 2, 1922.

1924   *America* received its premiere at 44th Street Theatre, New York, February 21.

1931   *The Struggle* received its premiere at the Rivoli, New York, December 10. It was the last film Griffith directed.

1936   Divorced Linda Arvidson; married Evelyn Marjorie Baldwin.

1947   Evelyn Baldwin opened divorce proceedings against DWG.

1948   DWG died July 23 in Hollywood, California.

My Early Life
by DAVID WARK GRIFFITH

About myself? The public cannot care about that topic; you cannot improve on what was written about a real man of note once: "He was born, he grew up, he slept a little, he ate a little, he worked a little, he loved a little—and then he died."

My family? I do come of good stock; my mother was a Shirley-Carter, my father was Colonel Jacob Wark Griffith of the Confederacy; old comrades of his in the war have told me he was known in the army as "Thunder Jake," [1] because he never went into a charge but what his voice could be heard above the din of guns and combat, urging on his men.

About the first thing I remember was my father's sword; he would put it on to amuse me. The first time I saw that sword was when my father played a joke on an old Negro, once his slave but who with the heads of four other Negro families refused to leave the plantation; those four families were four important factors in keeping the Griffith family poor.

Down South the men usually wore their hair rather long; this Negro who in our better days had been the plantation barber, had been taken to Louisville [Kentucky], ten or twelve miles from our home at Bairdstown, and had seen Northern men with their close-cropped hair; when he came back he got hold of my brother and cut his hair close, Northern-style.

When father saw this he pretended to be enraged; he went into the house, donned his old uniform, buckled on his sword and pistols, and had the Negro summoned.

Then, drawing the sword, he went through the technical cuts and

Excerpted from Henry Stephen Gordon, "The Story of David Wark Griffith," Photoplay, X (June, 1916), 35, 37, 162–65; (July, 1916) 124–29, 131–32. Gordon's work is a biography based on interviews with DWG. Footnotes supplied.

[1] Correctly: "Roaring Jake."

thrusts and slashes, threatening the darkey all the time with being cut up into mincemeat.

The old Uncle was scared pale, and I took it seriously myself until a wink and a smile from father enlightened me.

So that sword remains the first memory I have of existence.

We were all somewhat studious; father was a highly educated man, and an elder sister, Mattie, was a brilliantly cultured woman; she it was who gave the children their basic education; my parents always directed our studies and our thoughts toward the noble, the great in literature.

Mattie found in her father an intellect that met her requirements and a character that she adored; she never married, and would say, either jokingly or seriously, I was never certain which, but suspect the latter, that she never had found a man equal to her father, and that none of less quality would ever satisfy her as a husband.

Personally, I have not bothered about an ancestry; it is likely though that I was impressed in my childhood with certain family traditions which had come down through the mist of former generations; one was that *ap* Griffith, a Welsh Prince of Wales, was the founder of one side of the house, and that a Lord Brayington who revolted with Monmouth and later emigrated under duress to Virginia, was a founder of the other side of the American Griffiths.

I used to be told of a great-grandfather in Virginia, a stormy, fierce old man who refused to allow the word England to be spoken in his presence and who, as far as he could, barred his door to anything English.

My grandfather was a Captain David Griffith, who fought in 1812.

It happens I do know a lot about my father, from what I have been told by Southern soldiers. Colonel Polk Johnson told me of his regiment never having surrendered, and of his having been brevetted Brigadier General.

After I left home I walked through Kentucky and Tennessee once when I had a job as traveling correspondent and canvasser for the *Baptist Weekly,* and I met a man named, I think, Holly, who had served with father; I sat up all night with him listening to his stories about Colonel Griffith, whom he pronounced to be the bravest man he had ever seen in action.

"There was a Yankee supply train," said Holly, "that General Jo Wheeler had tried to capture with the regiment of another colonel, who had been driven off by the escort of the train; but the wagons were still within striking distance and Jo Wheeler very much wanted the bacon and ammunition they contained.

"An orderly called your father, and Jo said to him, 'Colonel, can you capture that Yankee wagon train?'

"Your father saluted and turned to go.

" 'Why don't you answer me, Colonel Griffith?' said General Jo.

" 'I'll answer you in five minutes,' said your father, and in that time he had the train on its way into our camp."

This incident I have found verified in Jefferson Davis' *Rise and Fall of The Confederacy*.

My first, and my last ambition, until Fate turned me into a picture man, was to be a writer. I determined on that when I was six years old. My father's sword and its early effect on my mind, his noble career, his wounds, for he was shot all to pieces, did impart a martial trend to my character, but there was no war, and the scholarly atmosphere of my home, I suppose, was responsible for my inclination to become a great literary man.

As soon as I was big enough I began my own personally conducted tour of Life. I went to Louisville and got a job as reporter on the *Courier-Journal*. I did not meet Marse Henry then. I wish I could have done something to make him notice me, but I did not; in some way I was put to work writing notes about theatrical matters. With my night police assignment and a general hunt for items, I determined to become a dramatist.

I received emphasis for that inspiration on seeing my first theatrical performance: in it was Pete Baker, who sang "America's National Game." Then I saw Julia Marlowe and Robert Taber in *Romola*.

That settled everything; I was to be a great dramatist. First it was necessary to secure some advice, so I called on the stage manager of the company of the Louisville theater and told him of my scheme of life.

He approved it thoroughly and solemnly; but he explained to me that no man could ever write a good play who was not an actor; he cited Shakespeare and Molière and Dion Boucicault and Gus Thomas, and as he was an authority I accepted his advice, thereby breaking a universal time-honored rule, and became an actor. I played in stock at Louisville, and after many ups and more downs, I had some good engagements.

My first part was the Clergyman in *Trilby*. I wasn't twenty then and I was paid eight dollars a week; then, later, I joined Walker Whiteside on tour through Iowa. I never have since then been in sympathy with Iowa ideas. After that I had a wide experience in characters, heavies, and leads.

It isn't all so long ago, yet I played a season with Helen Ware before she was discovered, and then with J. E. Dodson as Mauprat to his Richelieu, and was given a good notice by Alan Dale, which confirmed my suspicion that I was quite a good actor. It secured me as well an increase in salary. Then came a season with Nance O'Neill in

Shakespeare and Ibsen, in Boston; the reviewers gave me corking good notices there—but of course Shakespeare and Ibsen couldn't be roasted in Boston.

And reviewers are not always over-perceptive; there was a time when I was with Nance O'Neill and McKee Rankin right here in Los Angeles at the Mason theater, when Rankin was ill one night; I had been playing Magda's preacher lover, but when Rankin did not appear I was thrown into the part of the father. I stuffed out my clothes and went through the part with no change of name on the programme. The next morning's papers had most eulogistic notices of Mr. Rankin's thoroughly artistic acting, and the world looked very brilliant to me that day.

All the time my determination to be a dramatist was unshaken. I had, before getting deep in the theater, written two poems and a story; one of the poems I had sent to John Sleicher, editor of *Leslie's Weekly,* and he bought it; he paid me thirty-five dollars!

Ah! When *Leslie's* came out with my poem in it—that was the one day of all [my] life. It was called "To a Wild Duck." [2] It was a serious poem and not written on that subject because I was hungry. I bought a copy of the magazine and entered a subway train; I read the verses carelessly, registering indifference, and rolled the paper up and put it in my coat pocket; but—I couldn't stand it; it seemed as if everyone in the car would know I had written that poem, but I had to read it again; I pulled the paper out of my pocket, scanned the advertisements, and then as if by accident turned over to the poem and savored Victory again.

Can I remember it? Huh! let me see. The first line ran, "See how beautifully—" "See how beautifully—" No, it's all gone; I'm not even sure of the first line! And that was the happiest moment of my life—with what caused it forgotten. There might be something of a theme for a poem in that situation.

Naturally I wrote another poem, and sent it to *McClure's.* It came back; but you must pardon me, for a poet has to be very proud, while a picture man may be very modest; it came back, but with a personal letter from Colonel McClure saying the committee of five editors who passed on contributions had voted three to two against accepting the verses, but would I be good enough to send in some more.

I did not; but I sold a story that same month, and I began to write Sunday "Sup" stuff; I couldn't sell these specials myself, but I became acquainted with a very popular newspaper woman who was paid a high space rate; I would give her my stories and specials, and she would put her "byline" on them, sell them, and give me half the money.

---

[2] Correctly: "The Wild Duck."

And then I wrote my play; *the* play. It was called *A Fool and a Girl*.[3] I decided when it was finished that it was a good play, and I took it to James K. Hackett, who read it. "My boy," he said in his vigorous way, "this is one of the best plays I have ever read; I'll produce it!"

That day of the first poem appearing was as nothing; I must have been unbearably happy—until I met Mr. Hackett's stage director. He read the play; he turned to me when he had finished reading and said, "Your play's rotten. It will never go; the governor's blowing himself in by giving you a production. Why, man alive! You make characters talk and behave like real people. Rotten!"

Then he censored the play; he improved it; he deprived it of the sin of picturing real men and women on the stage and changed them into people of the theatrical mind.

But even at that it flivvered.

I was sure it was because the stage director had changed it, but—I knew Wilfred Lucas[4] then, who is with me now, and I asked him to read the play; he did so, but he has always refrained from telling me what he thought of it.

Come to think it over, there was something of a coincidence about that play and *The Clansman*;[5] the play had an important character who was a white man with a strain of Negro blood.

It was good training while that play was being put on; I lost twenty pounds of flesh a week, and my temper. I learned how to suffer, a knowledge that has often come in useful to me in the picture business. If you've ever had any disagreeable portion of your life, you understand the times of stress, the episodes where you licked or were licked; we look back upon having passed them—with keen joy. That is why Beranger's song about being happy at twenty in a garret always has been, and always will be beloved by all men.

This is a curious world we are in; while we are in it, we must be careful what we say, lest others say about us what is not careful, after we have gone. . . . I will not unfold all the secrets of my young life . . . and as to being a book agent, I refuse to incriminate myself. I stand mute. But I admit selling the *Encyclopedia Britannica*; that isn't a book; it is a freight commodity.

I did not sell very many—but even an occasional sale carried a very fat commission and enabled me to pack a meal ticket with my sample bindings, and to travel in railway cars in place of underneath them on a brakebeam.

I early learned to use means to discover the men who would likely

---

[3] Correctly: *The Fool and the Girl*. The manuscript is in the Library of Congress.
[4] He became one of DWG's leading Biograph actors.
[5] One of the literary sources of *The Birth of a Nation*. It was a novel by Thomas Dixon, Jr., first published in 1905 and subsequently dramatized.

want to listen to a seller of books; and had my friends and acquaintances trained to report to me information that might lead to a dicker.

There was a day when some one told some one else to tell me that Cousin Janie had said to Uncle Sawyer that Jim Dodson had heard Sam Roller from down river say that there was a man living at Burgoyne co'te house who owned a Bible and a dictionary; and who wanted an encyclopedia. . . .

My man lived in a country of pork and "sides" diet. It was a hard, grinding school I had been through; one that had taught me to think before acting. Knowing the value put on fresh meat in that region, I gambled quite a bit of my resources and bought a lot of good steaks. I could have used those steaks myself to advantage—but business is business, and strategy is strategy.

In a buggy with my bundle of steaks and my sample bindings and pages, we started one evening for my man.

There were not any roads thereabout when it rained. And it rained. We upset, we were bogged, but we managed to make progress until, while driving through a thick woods, a panther agilely dropped to the seat beside me from an overhanging tree, and I dropped out of the buggy. The beast had sniffed the odor of those steaks.

There was a pretty scrap while it lasted, but the panther was dislodged before the steaks were swallowed, and we drove on.

The farmer gave me shelter for the night, and for breakfast I presented my steaks, and before lunch I had made my sale. . . .

Success does make a fellow feel a bit proud, even if he realizes, as any honest, successful man must realize, how little there really is to achievement.

For a long time I was proudest over a journey I made from Minneapolis to my home on a capital of fifteen cents; and I still had the fifteen cents when I reached my destination.

That was one of my early adventures on "blind baggage" cars and brakebeams.

I had been acting, when the ghost which had limped sadly for some weeks failed to walk, even with crutches.

Luck had been favorable; I had made a living and had sent some money home, but back of the situation was a formidable oath I had taken when I struck out for myself that never would I ask for help from those I had left behind; as for meals and shelter, during a financial squall, that was different, and my thoughts and my feet turned toward the old plantation.

There is considerable alertness required to swing onto a "blind baggage" at the maximum of speed, to combine the minimum chance of discovery. When it happened that I was thrown off a train, I did odd jobs wherever I found myself, until the chance came rolling down the track again for another stage of the journey.

Along with the experience was a knowledge gained of the great army of vagabonds who constantly migrate simply from the love of wandering, the enjoyment of the savor of change. During those years I met in more or less intimacy all kinds and conditions of men—all kinds; what Kipling wrote of the Colonel's Lady and Judy O'Grady being just alike under the skin is equally true about the intellect of the "pike" and the university gentle; the yegg and the poet, the peripatetic and the stationary philosopher.

No matter how contorted one way or another the soul may be, the man is still a man, and with recognizable traits of relationship to all men.

Somewhat illustrative of the domination of circumstances over mental attitudes is another instance of—at the time—great pride to me.

This was an occasion around the warm cinders which had been drawn from the fireboxes of the locomotives in a roundhouse; the company was an assembly of tramps—hoboes they are called now—and I was given the center of the stage, the best place at the ashes, and called on for a monologic account of the longest uninterrupted blind baggage ride then on record, something over two hundred miles out of Chicago.

Louisville had again attracted me. A company had gone broke in Chicago and I with it. The way to arrive at a place, I had learned, is to start for it; so I walked from downtown in Chicago to Englewood, and there a train whizzed along so fast that the crew was not watching, feeling that no ticketless tourist would take the chance. This one did, and landed safely. It was a wild night, stormy and freezing; the crew of the train stuck to their snug quarters, not knowing their flying bailiwick had been invaded, until one brakeman made a perfunctory inspection. I also had grown careless from long immunity and sleepiness.

Consciousness returned violently when I was assailed by two bulging red fists, accompanied by much language. We made a fairly even match; but a second brakeman hovered along and then it was all over. I reposed gratefully on a snow bank with many minor injuries to my person and a realization that Louisville was a great deal farther away than when I had been in Chicago.

Something led me to walk a bit, and I came to the roundhouse, the pile of warm cinders, and the gallant company of the Knights of Disindustry. When my story was heard there was acclaim, unenvious and generous comment, and the warmest place by the cinders.

Which is generally more than a man is given when he succeeds with people who are—not hoboes. . . .

Nothing had changed my decision to be the world's greatest literary man, and I felt that as a preparatory study, before I could have the world of letters at my feet, it might be useful to know a little more about certain phases of life commonly unfamiliar.

My other adventures had been made of necessity; this was one of choice, for the knowledge of the working man—the toiler—I thought would be valuable.

There was no financial need spurring me to ride hard over the rough spots in the highway of existence; a comfortable sum of a few hundred dollars had been accumulated by some occasional good fortune in the theatre, and my duties toward those at home had been met.

To be a puddler in a foundry, to do the real muscle-stretching, bone-bending work, and to live among the men who did such work, was my ambition, and naturally I went to Tonawanda. I didn't work at puddling first, but shoveling ore out of a ship's hold into the crane buckets.

There were no union restrictions as to hours, or anything; the pay was not by the day but by the piece; so much money for every ton of ore shoveled; it was good enough pay, so good that if a man would work until he dropped in his tracks he could pick up twenty dollars or so at a piece.

It was work under tremendous competitive conditions; I mean the competition of emulation.

Men would shovel down in that grimy, stuffy hold until they dropped in their tracks from utter exhaustion; then they would be chucked into one of the steel buckets, hoisted to the deck, and flung to one side, to come to, or go to, as they listed.

Under that stint system that work was probably the hardest in the world; for young men it was beautifully healthful; it was not long before I found myself capable of shoveling ore for twenty-four hours at a stretch. In some traits the men were as hard and exhausting as the life; they were naturally circumscribed, and if their daily existence was an orgy of labor, their life when released from toil was just as strenuous in their efforts to win relief.

So, in one way or another, under this or that circumstance, my life flowed on, with no approachment to that laurel wreath of literature; I was acting most of the time, and essaying a few other lines of livelihood. . . . [As to the ore-shoveling] it was corking good. I feel the benefit of it every day I live; it gave me physical resiliency, fortitude, and some little muscle which has been of particular value to me many times.

Every phase of life is good for you if you face it all rightly, with fine cheer.

For tramps, artists, ironworkers, actors, writers—all of us—are alike in our souls; it was in knowing all manner of men that I derived my most useful education.

And then came the photoplay.

It happened very casually, as most events do occur, for it proved to be an event to me. It was one day in Chicago when with a friend I was knocking about town with no purpose in immediate view; he suggested that we go to a picture show.

Never having seen one, the suggestion was inviting. We went; it was some boreful affair, exactly what, I have forgotten; my friend liked it greatly, but I found it silly, tiresome, inexcusable. It was in no way worthwhile.

But the great interest the audience evinced impressed me, and made me think; it seemed that if a thing which could attract the public as that picture did were to be done, it should be done better.

"What did you think of it?" asked my comrade.

"That any man who enjoys such a thing should be shot at sunrise," was my response.

He looked at me in wonder and talked on, explaining why the picture was great; and when we went out he called my attention to the line of people waiting to enter the theater.

Things did not go very well just then for me; I found myself out of work, and all the time pictures were being talked of, and unconsciously that interested audience and the line of people outside stuck in my mind.

Probably then, as now, there was no egotism in my thinking that I could write far better scenarios than were being shown, and that the acting of the pictures could be improved.

As to whether I seriously at that time gave any studied effort to the new profession, I cannot say; it is probable that unconsciously I gave it all considerably more attention than I then realized. For it was a prospect, and the feeling that you can do something perhaps a little better than it is being done makes interest acutely active.

Finally I wrote a scenario and took it to the Edison studio.[6] I left it and was told I would receive an answer.

That scenario is still on file there, I presume; I never heard anything of it since.

[6] It was a synopsis of *La Tosca* and was rejected by Edwin S. Porter because it contained too many scenes.

Griffith Directs
His First Movie
by LINDA ARVIDSON

Considering the chaotic condition of things in the studio as a result of Mr. McCutcheon's illness, it was a propitious time to take heed and get on the tricks of this movie business.[1] To David Griffith the direction was insufferably careless, the acting the same, and in the lingering bitterness over his play's failure he gritted his teeth and decided that if he ever got a chance he certainly could direct these dinky movies.

The studio was so without a head these days that even Henry Norton Marvin, our vice-president and general manager, occasionally helped out in the directing. He had directed a mutoscope[2] called "A Studio Party" in which my husband and I had made a joint appearance.

With the place now "runnin' wild," Mr. Marvin wondered whom he'd better take a chance on next.

He put the odds on Mr. Stanner E. V. Taylor.[3]

In the studio, one day shortly after my initiation, Mr. Taylor approached me and asked if I could play a lead in a melodrama he was

From Linda Arvidson (Mrs. D. W. Griffith), When the Movies Were Young (New York: Dutton, 1925), Chapter VII, pp. 45–52. Footnotes supplied.

[1] George "Old Man" McCutcheon, director of productions at the Biograph company. Wallace, his eldest son, directed films for the same company. Subsequently, "Wally" became the husband of Serial Queen, Pearl White.

[2] Mutoscopes were a series of still photographs made for use in the Mutoscope, a peep-show device that rivalled Edison's Kinetoscope. Inside the Mutoscope the still photographs were flicked at a speed sufficient to produce the effect of persistence of vision—and thereby of pictures in motion. The Biograph Company was an outgrowth of a company originally formed to make Mutoscopes. See further Gordon Hendricks, *Beginnings of the Biograph* (New York: The Beginnings of the American Film, 1964).

[3] A journalist who became a leading screenwriter for the Biograph Company. He wrote many of DWG's film stories, including the story for Griffith's first film as a director: *The Adventures of Dollie* (1908).

to direct. A lead in a melodrama—with a brief stage career that had been confined to winsome ingénues! But I bravely said, "Oh, yes, yes, indeed I can." . . .

The picture—the only one Mr. Taylor directed—lacked continuity. Upstairs in his executive office, Mr. Henry Norton Marvin was walking the floor and wondering what about it. Why couldn't they get somewhere with these movies? Another man fallen down on the job. Genial Arthur Marvin, H. N.'s brother, and Billy Bitzer's assistant at the camera, was being catechized as to whether he had noticed any promising material about the studio.

"Well," drawled the genial Arthur, "I don't know. They're a funny lot, these actors, but there's one young man, there's one actor seems to have ideas. You might try him."

"You think he might get by, eh?"

"Well, I don't think you'd lose much by trying him."

"What's his name? I'll send for him."

"Griffith. Lawrence Griffith."

Later that day a cadaverous-looking young man was closeted with the vice-president in the vice-president's dignified quarters.

"My brother tells me you appear to be rather interested in the pictures, Mr. Griffith; how would you like to direct one?"

Mr. Griffith rose from his chair, took three steps to the window, and gazed out into space.

"Think you'd like to try it, Mr. Griffith?"

No response—only more gazing into space.

"We'll make it as easy as we can for you, Mr. Griffith, if you decide you'd like to try."

More gazing into space. And finally this: "I appreciate your confidence in me, Mr. Marvin, but there is just this to it. I've had rather rough sledding the last few years and you see I'm married; I have responsibilities and I cannot afford to take chances; I think they rather like me around here as an actor. Now if I take this picture-directing over and fall down, then you see I'll be out my acting job, and you know I wouldn't like that; I don't want to lose my job as an actor down here."

"Otherwise you'd be willing to direct a picture for us?"

"Oh, yes, indeed I would."

"Then if I promise that if you fall down as a director, you can have your acting job back, you will put on a moving picture for us?"

"Yes, then I'd be willing."

It was called *The Adventures of Dolly* [sic].[4]

---

[4] Correctly: *The Adventures of Dollie*. According to R. M. Henderson the film was produced during June 18–19 and released July 14, 1908. It totalled 713 feet.

Gossip around the studio had it that the story was a "lemon." Preceding directors at the studio had sidestepped it. *Dolly,* in the course of the story, is nailed into a barrel by the gypsies who steal her; the barrel [is] secreted in the gypsy wagon; the horses start off at breakneck speed; the barrel falls off the wagon, rolls into the stream, floats over a waterfall, shoots the rapids, and finally emerges into a quiet pool where some boys, fishing, haul it ashore, hear the child's cries, open the barrel, and rescue *Dolly.*

Not a very simple job for an amateur. But David Griffith wasn't worried. He could go back to acting were the picture no good. Mr. Arthur Marvin was assigned as cameraman. There were needed for the cast: *Dolly,* her mother and father, the gypsy man, the gypsy man's wife, and two small boys.

Upstairs in the tiny projection room pictures were being run for Mr. Griffith's enlightenment. He was seeing what Biograph movies looked like. Saw some of old man McCutcheon's, and some of Wally McCutcheon's, and Stanner E. V. Taylor's one and only.

That evening he said to me: "You'll play the lead in my first picture—not because you're my wife—but because you're a good actress."

"Oh, did you see Mr. Taylor's picture?"

"Yes."

"How was it?"

"Not bad, but it don't hang together. Good acting; you're good, quite surprised me. No one I can use for a husband though. I must have some one who *looks* like a 'husband'—who looks as though he owned more than a cigarette. I heard around the studio that they were going to hand me a bunch of lemons for actors."

So, dashing madly here and there for a father for little *Dolly,* Mr. Griffith saw coming down Broadway a young man of smiling countenance—just the man—his very ideal. Of course, he must be an actor. There was no time for hesitation.

"Pardon me, but would you care to act in a moving picture? I am going to direct a moving picture, and I have a part that suits you exactly."

"Moving pictures, did you say? Picture acting? I am sure I don't know what you are talking about. I don't know anything about picture acting."

"You don't need to know—just meet me at the Grand Central Depot at nine o'clock tomorrow morning."

And so Arthur Johnson became a movie actor.

To my mind no personality has since flickered upon the screen with quite the charm, lovableness, and magnetic humor that were his. He never acquired affectations, which made him a rare person indeed, considering the tremendous popularity that became his and the world of affectation in which he lived.

For the gypsy man Mr. Griffith selected Charles Inslee, an excellent actor whom he had known on the Coast. Mr. Inslee was a temperamental sort, but Mr. Griffith knew how to handle him. So with Mrs. Gebhardt for the gypsy wife, Mr. Griffith completed his cast without using a single one of the "lemons" that were to have been wished upon him; and as there were only outdoor sets in *The Adventures* he did not have any of the "lemons" around to make comments.

Even the business of the barrel proved to be no insurmountable difficulty. Yards and yards of piano-wire were attached, which, manipulated from the shore, kept the barrel somewhat in focus. The one perturbed person was our cameraman, who even though middle-aged and heavy, time and time again had to jump about, in and out of the stream, grabbing tripod and clumsy camera, trying to keep up with the floating barrel.

We went to Sound Beach, Connecticut, to take *The Adventures*.

It was a lovely place, I thought. The black-eyed Susans were all a-bloom, and everywhere was green grass although it was nearly midsummer. We spent almost a week working on *The Adventures,* for the mechanical scenes took time, and—joy!—between us we were making ten dollars a day as long as the picture lasted.

And then who could tell!

"If the photography is there, the picture will be all right; if it looks as good on the negative as it looked while we were taking it, it ought to get by," opined the director.

From out of the secrecy of the dark room came Arthur Marvin, nonchalantly swinging a short strip of film.

"How is it?"

"Looks pretty good, nice and sharp."

"Think it's all right?"

"Yeh, think it is."

Hopeful hours interspersed with anxious moments crowded the succeeding days. By the time the picture was developed, printed, and titled, we were well-nigh emotionally exhausted. What would they say upstairs? What *would* they say?

In the darkened little projection room they sat.

On the screen was being shown *The Adventures of Dolly*.

No sound but the buzz and whir of the projection machine. The seven hundred and thirteen feet of the *Adventures* were reeled off. Silence. Then Mr. Marvin spoke:

"That's it—that's something like it—at last!"

Afterwards, upstairs in the executive offices, Mr. Marvin and Mr. Dougherty talked it over, and they concluded that if the next picture were half as good, Lawrence Griffith was the man they wanted. The next picture really turned out better.

The world's première of *The Adventures of Dolly* was held at Keith and Proctor's Theatre, Union Square, July 14, 1908. What a day it was at the studio! However did we work, thinking of what the night held? But as the longest day ends, so did this one. No time to get home and pretty-up for the party. With what meager facilities the porcelain basin and makeup shelf in the dressing room offered, we managed; rubbed off the grease paint and slapped on some powder; gave the hair a pat and a twist; at Silsbee's on Sixth Avenue and Fourteenth Street, we picked up nourishment; and then we beat it to Union Square.

A world's première indeed—a tremendously important night to so many people who didn't know it. No taxis—not one private car drew up at the curb. The house filled up from passers-by—frequenters of Union Square—lured by a ten-cent entertainment. These were the people to be pleased—they who had paid out their little nickels and dimes. So when they sat through *Dolly*'s seven hundred feet, interested, and not a snore was to be heard, we concluded we'd had a successful opening night.

The contract was drawn for one year. It called for forty-five dollars per week with a royalty of a mill a foot on all film sold. Mr. Marvin thought it rather foolish to accept so small a salary and assured my husband the percentage would amount to nothing whatever right off. But David was willing—rather more than willing—to gamble on himself. And he gambled rather well this time. For, the first year his royalty check went from practically nothing to four and five hundred dollars a month—before the end of the year.

Wonderful it was—too good to be true. Although, had he known then that for evermore, through weeks and months and years, it was to be movies, movies, nothing but movies, David Griffith would probably then and there have chucked the job, or, keeping it, would have wept bitter, bitter tears.

D. W. Griffith, Producer of
The World's Biggest Picture
Interview with D. W. GRIFFITH

If your mental picture of "Dave" Griffith is that of a man of the bludgeon type, you are mistaken. The biggest man in the moving picture business today is a curious mingling of the man of leisure, man of the world, and the dreaming poet.

Yet his quarrel with life is that "They," the indeterminate word with which he includes people and conditions of today, "keep him running around." He clutched two telegrams that looked, as he said, like the afternoon edition of newspapers, as he talked to the interviewer across the luncheon table at a Broadway hotel and confided that the only man on earth of whom he is afraid, his secretary, might enter the room any minute.

"It's amazing the way that man keeps me running around," he said. "I hope he's taking a nap, a nice long one, that will keep him away from me all afternoon." He has the poet's quality of wanting to be left alone while he is dreaming his poet's dreams and getting a little pleasure in a good joke or a story, and those pestiferous persons who keep you "running around" sadly interfere with both.

Yet, in defiance of these leanings, and in large part because of them, he is conceded to be the greatest producer of motion pictures in the world. The most poetic, the most daring, the most artistic and the most stupendous works have had their inception in his brain and been worked out under his direction. This week there will be shown at the Liberty Theatre[1] the largest film drama yet conceived, a film 13,058 feet long, a three-hour entertainment, during which no less than 18,000 people come before the eyes.

Originally published in New York American, *February 28, 1915,* City Life and Dramatic section, *p. 9. Footnotes supplied.*

[1] In New York City, March 3, 1915.

"Why call it *The Birth of a Nation?*" the interviewer asked.

"Because it is," was the sufficient answer from the lean, smiling man across the table, who has been called the "David Belasco of the Motion Pictures." "The Civil War was fought fifty years ago. But the real nation has only existed the last fifteen or twenty years, for there can exist no union without sympathy and oneness of sentiment. While Thomas Dixon's novel, *The Clansman,* is the basis of the play, we don't get to that until the film is half done. The author himself was good enough to say that the novel was so small a part of it that he thought it should not be considered. He said that in his novel he had taken a small section of the subject, a racial war. But we have gone back to the Civil War itself. We have shown the burning of Atlanta and the assassination of Lincoln. The birth of the nation began, according to an authority,[2] with the Ku Klux Klans, and we have shown that. We are using many veterans who served in the war."

"What do you think is the biggest thing in the big picture?"

"The burning of Atlanta, perhaps. More probably the battle of Petersburg, with the armies in the trenches. Yes, that is the biggest."

"And the littlest?"

"The littlest thing, in one sense, is the sigh of General Lee as the papers of surrender were signed. And, too, the fact that they had to pass the pen around and dip it into several bottles before they could get enough ink to sign it.

"We took some of the pictures in the region around Los Angeles, some of them in Mexico, others in various southern states. I traveled 15,000 miles in making the picture."

"Is it your greatest work, and are you content with it?"

"It is the biggest thing I have undertaken, but I shall not be satisfied until I do something else. I can see the mistakes in this. I am, like all other human beings, aiming at perfection."

"And that is the reason we never achieve our ambitions. But *The Birth of a Nation* received very high praise from high quarters in Washington."

"Yes, I was gratified when a man we all revere, or ought to, said it teaches history by lightning."[3]

"They say a great many things about you. One is that you came into the world of moving pictures when they were despised, and that you raised them to dignity. I have even heard that if it hadn't been for the transfusion of your blood into it the motion picture art would have died."

[2] Presumably Woodrow Wilson, in Volume V of his *A History of the American People* (New York, 1902). See further Seymour Stern's note on DWG's sources, *Film Culture,* no. 36 (Spring–Summer 1965), pp. 34–36.

[3] An apocryphal remark attributed to Woodrow Wilson.

"If that were true I wouldn't be ashamed of it. I believe in the motion picture not only as a means of amusement, but as a moral and educational force. Do you know that there has been less drinking in the past five years, and that it is because of motion pictures? It is absolutely true. No man drinks for the sake of drinking. He drinks because he has no place to go. Man is a moving animal. The bigger the man the more he has need of activity. It isn't so with women. Their natures are different. The motion pictures give man a place to go beside the saloons. He drops in to see a picture. He has been somewhere. He has seen something. He comes out and goes home in a different state than if he had gone to a saloon. The domestic unities are preserved.

"As for improprieties in motion pictures, they do not exist. What motion pictures have you seen that revealed the anatomical wonders that a Broadway musical comedy or burlesque show frankly discloses? I recall no motion picture that deals in any way with the nude save one, and that should never have been produced. There was once the claim that the playhouses were kept too dark for propriety. That criticism was made long ago, and it was never true. The requirements for motion picture lighting are such that you must be able to see a face twenty feet from the picture.

"If I had a growing son I should be willing to let him see motion pictures as he liked, because I believe they would be an invaluable aid to his education. They would stimulate his imagination, without which no one will go far. They would also give him a fund of knowledge, history and otherwise, and all good. And they would shape his character along the most rigid plane of human conduct. In moving pictures the code of conduct is hard and fast. No one need fear that it will deviate from the Puritan plane."

"And the physical side of it? When will motion pictures be so made that they will not strain the eyes?"

"They have improved greatly in that respect within a year. They are constantly improving. Even now some of them do not tire the eyes any more than do the figures in a play."

"What is your vision of the motion pictures of the future?"

"I expect that in five years pictures will be made at a cost of a million dollars. *The Birth of a Nation* cost half a million. And I expect audiences will pay not merely what they are paying for a legitimate drama today, but as much as they pay for grand opera—five dollars a seat."

COMMENTARY
by D. W. Griffith

Moving Pictures Can Get Nothing from the Stage

◆◆◆

Moving pictures can get nothing from the so-called legitimate stage because American directors and playwrights have nothing to offer. The former are, for the most part, conventional and care nothing for natural acting. They don't know how to make use of even the material they have, limited as that is. Of course, there are a few, a very few, exceptions. As for American playwrights, we can get our ideas from the same sources they do. We need to depend on the stage for our actors and actresses least of all. How many of them make you believe they are real human beings? No, they "act," that is, they use a lot of gestures and make a lot of sounds such as are never seen or heard anywhere else. For range and delicacy, the development of character, the quick transition from one mood to another, I don't know an actress now on the American stage, I don't care how great her reputation, who can begin to touch the work of some of the motion picture actresses. And I'll give you the names if you want them.

As far as the public is concerned, there is no real competition between the stage and the motion picture. It doesn't exist. The latter makes an appeal which the former never has and never can hope to meet, not only because of its physical limitations, but because most of its managers, directors, and actors are bound by tradition. They don't know human nature and they don't care to find out about it. James A. Herne,[1] who wrote plays with real people in them, is only just beginning to be rightly appreciated years after his death. Wonderful Mrs. Fiske is, of course, one of the exceptions, too.

From "A Poet Who Writes on Motion Picture Film," The Theatre, *XIX (June, 1914), pp. 311–12, 314, 316. Footnote supplied.*

[1] James A. Herne (1839–1901); perhaps his most notable realist dramas are *Margaret Fleming* (1890) and *Shore Acres* (1892).

Griffith's Replies to Two Questions

◆◆

You ask me: "Do you think the stage and its craft are the best means of productivity for the cameraman?" No, I do not. The stage is a development of centuries, based on certain fixed conditions and within prescribed limits. It is needless to point out what these are. The motion picture, although a growth of only a few years, is boundless in its scope and endless in its possibilities. The whole world is its stage, and time without end its limitations. In the use of speech alone it is at a disadvantage, but the other advantages of the motion picture over the stage are so numerous and powerful that we can well afford to grant the stage this one point of superiority. The conditions of the two arts being so different, it follows that the requirements are equally dissimilar. Stage craft and stage people are out of place in the intense realism of motion-picture expression, but it may well be that a little motion-picture realism would be of immense advantage to the stage.

To your second question, "After the plays of other days are exhausted, who will supply the needs of thirty thousand theatres?" I would refer you to the opinion expressed in the foregoing paragraph. The plays of other days are not essential to the motion picture, and I am not sure that they are not proving a positive harm. If motion picture producers had no access to stage plays, they would be obliged to depend upon their own authors for their material, and, since the picture dramas that would thus result would be composed entirely for picture production, they could not fail to much more nearly reach a perfection of art than could ever be hoped for while writers and directors are trying in vain to twist stage dramas into condition for picture use. When the plays of other days, and of these days are exhausted, as they will be, motion pictures will come into their own. They are valued now only for advertising purposes, and, when a stage play is reproduced in pictures with any success, it is inevitably found that often the plot and always the manner of treatment have been entirely departed from.

From Robert Grau, The Theatre of Science *(New York, 1914), pp. 85–87.*

Some Prophecies: Film and Theatre, Screenwriting, Education

◈◈◈

The regular theatre . . . will, of course, always exist, but not, I believe, as now. The [moving] pictures will utterly eliminate from the regular theatre all the spectacular features of production. Plays will never again appeal to the public for their scenery, or their numbers of actors and supernumeraries. Pictures have replaced all that.

The only plays that the public will care to see in the regular theatre will be the intimate, quiet plays that can be staged in one or two settings within four walls, and in which the setting is unimportant, while the drama will be largely subjective. Objective drama, the so-called melodrama, will be entirely absorbed in the pictures. . . .

We are coming to pay more and more attention to the stories we use on the screen. The art of writing for the pictures is developing almost as rapidly as the art of acting for them. And the great rewards to be gained there by a writer will be a powerful incentive for him to learn to tell his story more crisply, more tellingly, more alluringly, than he ever could, even in the best spoken drama. . . .

The human race will think more rapidly, more intelligently, more comprehensively than it ever did. It will see everything—positively everything.

That, I believe, is the chief reason that the American public is so hungry for motion pictures and so loyal to a good one when it comes along. They have the good old American faculty of wanting to be "shown" things. We don't "talk" about things happening, or describe how a thing looks; we actually show it—vividly, completely, convincingly. It is the ever-present, realistic, actual now that "gets" the great American public, and nothing ever devised by the mind of man can show it like moving pictures. . . .

The time will come, and in less than ten years . . . where the children in the public schools will be taught practically everything by moving pictures. Certainly they will never be obliged to read history again.

From D. W. Griffith, "Five Dollar 'Movies' Prophesied," The Editor *(April 24, 1915), pp. 407–10.*

Imagine a public library of the near future, for instance. There will be long rows of boxes or pillars, properly classified and indexed, of course. At each box a push button and before each box a seat. Suppose you wish to "read up" on a certain episode in Napoleon's life. Instead of consulting all the authorities, wading laboriously through a host of books, and ending bewildered, without a clear idea of exactly what did happen and confused at every point by conflicting opinions about what did happen, you will merely seat yourself at a properly adjusted window, in a scientifically prepared room, press the button, and actually see what happened.

There will be no opinions expressed. You will merely be present at the making of history. All the work of writing, revising, collating, and reproducing will have been carefully attended to by a corps of recognized experts, and you will have received a vivid and complete expression.

Everything except the three R's, the arts, and possibly the mental sciences can be taught in this way—physiology, chemistry, biology, botany, physics, and history in all its branches. . . .

Working for the Biograph Company

◆◆

Those early Biograph days were the most picturesque since the time of Molière and of Villon; true, there was no "sleeping under the end of a star" and there were no medieval vagrancy classifications for us; but there were the freedom, the change of scene, and the coursing about the country as Romans, pirates, royalty, great lovers, and great villains; some days we would be playing at Commodore Benedict's great country place up the Sound, or at Seton-Thompson's home, and again would be chasing down a punch scene on the Bowery or in the midst of the human sewer seepage of Rivington Street.

There was then unusual interest in the new form of amusement, the Movies; we were generally treated with respect and given welcome and

From Henry Stephen Gordon, "The Story of David Wark Griffith," Photoplay *(June–November, 1916). Biography based on interviews with DWG. Footnotes supplied.*

the consideration due to artists; but there were the sharp contrasts which give to life its personal dramatic fillip.

It was in one of these expeditions that I discovered Cuddybackville,[1] the most beautiful, altogether the loveliest spot in America . . . somewhere about a hundred miles from New York; I don't think you can find it in a gazetteer for I don't even know how to spell the name; I don't want it found, and spoiled, for I hope some time to see it again, still untroubled by trippers, unmoved by flying tissue-paper picnic napkins, untainted by cigarette-smoked advanced minds.

Cuddybackville is a place where Goldsmith could have written as he did of Auburn; which Tennyson would have peopled with the lovely majesty of romance; and where in our small way we found a perfect "location" for scenes for a film of *The Last of the Mohicans*;[2] the film is now and happily forgotten, but none of that company can ever forget Cuddybackville.

That place illustrated what was the charm of that life; there we were in the dress and the demeanor of the Leather Stocking days, acting on a stage that was set by the One stage director to a perfection that even Cooper could not have described.

There is a quality about the light there, particularly a twilight that I have never found elsewhere; it is transcendently illuminative for [moving] pictures. . . .

I found that picture-makers were following as best they could the theory of the stage. A story was to be told in pictures, and it was told in regular stage progression; it is bad stage technique to repeat; it would be bad stage technique to have an actor show only his face; there are infinite numbers of things we do in pictures that would be absurdities on the stage, and I decided that to do with the camera only what was done on the stage was equally absurd.

My first anarchistic effort was what we now call the "close-up." This made me laughed at again at first; but I had become used to jeers, and feeling I was right I kept at it; what caused the fizzle at first was that in my attempt to get the actors closer to the camera I misjudged distance and their heads did not show in the film.[3] . . .

[1] Near Port Jervis, on the border of New York and New Jersey.

[2] DWG's first film at Cuddybackville was *The Mended Lute* ("A stirring Romance of the Dakotas") released August 5, 1909. The film DWG recalls was actually a version of Cooper's Natty Bumppo stories, titled *Leather Stocking*, made at Cuddybackville and released September 27, 1909. See further R. M. Henderson, *D. W. Griffith: The Years at Biograph* (New York: Farrar, Straus and Giroux, 1970), pp. 76–86.

[3] DWG first moved the camera closer to his actors to show their reactions in detail in *For Love of Gold* (1908). According to Linda Arvidson (Mrs. Griffith), DWG's *After Many Years*, made later in 1908, contained the first "dramatic close-up" and the first cutback. See Linda Arvidson, *When the Movies Were Young* (New York: Dutton, 1925), Chapter IX.

The "switchback" enabled me to follow the story with exactitude and at the same time preserve in the mind of the spectator an unimpaired continuity, with added emphasis.[4]

For example, a character says to another: "I hate you"; you show the speaker's face, and then switch in the face of the man to whom the remark is made with its expression, and then perhaps a bit of a previous scene which laid the foundation for the hatred.

That method is now used in a million different manners, and in a way has possibly transformed the entire procedure of picture-making. . . .

In making *Just Gold* [5] I began to seek after atmosphere and effects, and the clue to causes. If I have had a measure of success, possibly that effort was responsible largely, for it started me in the right direction.

It was in making a picture with Mary Pickford that I believe she first met Owen Moore. It seems to me that the title of the picture was *The Red Man,* or something like it.[6]

At any rate it was in this we perfected the fade-in and fade-out effect, after a lot of experimenting.

This received most severe criticism, which continued as late as my *Judith* picture. That was made, I think, about three years ago,[7] and now that method is being used probably to excess. . . .

Ingomar with Florence Lawrence followed soon, and that went far toward sustaining all of my ideas which had been used in its making.[8] As I recall it, Miss Lawrence also had a romance created from that picture and married Harry Sutter, who became quite as distinguished as a director as was she as an actress. . . .

Those were the days of the half-reels; we made two pictures a week. It was something of a struggle to get them out, especially at the time when everyone was calling me crazy, and not only calling, but believing I was crazy. Or worse, a simple fool.

Why, often we have got a picture completed in two days. Now we take that much time or more just to decide on the costumes we will use.

---

[4] DWG used "switchback" to signify both flashback and cross-cutting in developing parallel action. See further R. M. Henderson, op. cit., p. 165.

[5] Released May 24, 1913. Griffith has evidently confused this film with his earlier *For Love of Gold,* released August 21, 1908.

[6] DWG made *The Redman and the Child* (1908), *The Red Girl* (1908), and *The Redman's View* (1909), but Owen Moore and Mary Pickford do not appear to have acted in any of these pictures. Nothing is known of a DWG film titled *The Red Man.* The first appearance of Owen Moore and Mary Pickford in the same film was evidently in DWG's *1776* or *The Hessian Renegades* (1909).

[7] *Judith of Bethulia,* made in 1913 and released March 7, 1914. Bitzer was the cameraman; the picture was in four reels.

[8] *The Barbarian—Ingomar* (1908).

Of course it hurts my sense of modesty to admit the fact, but it is true that in a few months Biograph pictures were considered far away the best.

Newspapers began to notice them voluntarily, as a matter of general interest; the Biograph was quickly taken in by the General Film Company, which meant the largest organization and most profitable before or since.

In 1911 the Motion Picture Patents Company, an adjunct of the General Film Company, earned 1,700 percent on its capital stock, according to certified reports.

A few two-reel pictures began to be seen; under that regime we would make one reel one week and the other the next week.[9] This was possibly the beginning of the serial idea of pictures.

My largest picture with the Biograph was *Judith*,[10] a four-reel picture which I thought immense at the time. I made that with Blanche Sweet. She with Mary Pickford, in fact all the picture actresses of note, then came to the screen from the stage.

One of my early pictures I did like was *When Pippa Passes*.[11] We put that on in three days; considerably less time, I fancy, than Browning used in writing the poem. We had to do everything at once.

Then came *Enoch Arden, The Blot on the 'Scutcheon*,[12] *Taming of the Shrew*,[13] *Lines of White on a Sullen Sea*,[14] and others; these were all one-reels, and all were made before *Judith*.[15]

[9] DWG's first two-reeler, *Enoch Arden* (1911), was actually released for showing as two separate reels.

[10] *Judith of Bethulia* (1913), see above, note 7. This was Griffith's last picture for the Biograph Company.

[11] *Pippa Passes*, or *The Song of Conscience* (1909). The film is notable (a) for its lighting innovations (see Henderson, op. cit., pp. 83–85), and (b) for being the first film reviewed by *The New York Times* (October 10, 1909).

[12] *A Blot on the 'Scutcheon* (1911).

[13] *The Taming of the Shrew* (1908).

[14] *Lines of White on a Sullen Sea* (1909). The title was taken from a poem by William Carleton.

[15] See note 7.

How I Made The Birth of a Nation

◆◇◆

When Mr. Woods[1] suggested *The Clansman*[2] to me as a subject it hit me hard; I hoped at once that it could be done, for the story of the South had been absorbed into the very fibre of my being.

Mr. Dixon wrote to me suggesting the project, and I reread the book at once.

There had been a picture made by another concern, but this had been a failure;[3] as the theme developed in my mind, it fascinated me until I arrived at the point where I had to make the picture; if I had known that the result would mean disaster I do not think it would have mattered to me; truly I never was sure that the result would be a success; that first night showing at the Auditorium,[4] if anyone had offered me just a shade over what it had cost, I would have taken the money just as quickly as I could reach for it.

There were several months lost in the negotiations for the rights, as by that time other producers had gained the same idea, like myself, undeterred by one failure having already been made.

As I studied the book, stronger and stronger came to work the traditions I had learned as a child; all that my father had told me. That sword I told you about[5] became a flashing vision. Gradually came back

Excerpted from Henry Stephen Gordon, "The Story of David Wark Griffith," Photoplay, X (October, 1916), 90–94. Gordon's work is a biography based on interviews with DWG. Footnotes supplied.

[1] Frank E. Woods, film critic of *The Dramatic Mirror* and screenwriter for the Biograph Company.

[2] *The Clansman: An Historical Romance of the Ku Klux Klan,* by Thomas Dixon, Jr. (a novel). First published in 1905.

[3] Prior to 1912 the Kinemacolor Company of America began filming a version of the stage production of *The Clansman.* This film version was never completed, but one of the continuity writers for the production was Frank E. Woods who later suggested to DWG the idea of making a film of *The Clansman.*

[4] February 8, 1915, at Clune's Auditorium, Los Angeles, California. The film was then titled *The Clansman.* The title was changed to *The Birth of a Nation* for the New York premiere, Liberty Theatre, March 3, 1915. After the first New York showings, some 558 feet of film were removed by the censors, leaving 12,500 feet of the original release length of 13,058 feet.

[5] See this anthology, pp. 13–14.

to my memory the stories a cousin, one Thurston Griffith, had told me of the "Ku Klux Klan," and that regional impulse that comes to all men from the earth where they had their being stirred potently at my imagination.

But there was nothing of personal exhilaration required to make a picture out of that theme; few others like it in subject and power can be found, for it had all the deep incisive emotionalism of the highest patriotic sentiment.

I wouldn't say that the story part of that picture can ever be excelled, but as for the picture itself, there will be others made that will make it appear archaic in comparison.

For the feature picture has just begun to come into its own; my personal idea is that the minor pictures have had their day; the two- and three- and four-reel ones are passing, if not gone.

As I worked, the commercial side of the venture was lost to my view; I felt driven to tell the story—the truth about the South, touched by its eternal romance which I had learned to know so well.

I may be pardoned for saying that now I believe I did succeed in a measure in accomplishing that ambition.

It all grew as we went! I had no scenario, and never looked again at some few notes I made as I read the book, and which I read to my company before we began. Naturally the whole story was firmly in my mind, and possibly the personal exuberance of which I have told you enabled me to amplify and to implant in the scenes something of the deep feeling I experienced in that epoch that had meant everything, and then had left nothing to my nearest, my kin, and those about me.

There was not a stage star in my company; "Little Colonel" [Henry] Walthall had been out with Henry Miller, and had achieved some reputation, though by no means of stellar sort. Possibly he felt a bit of the impulse of locality, for his father was a Confederate colonel.

Miriam Cooper, the elder Cameron sister, was a perfect type of the beauty prevalent below the Mason and Dixon line, and Mae Marsh was from the same part of the Union, while Spottiswoode Aitken—"Dr. Cameron"—was related to a large group of distinguished Southern families.

These people were not picked because of place of birth or of their personal feeling about the story; still, it was a fortunate incident that they were what they were; it is hard to figure exactly how far what [is] bred in the bone will shine through the mind.

The casting frankly was all done by types; Miss Cooper, for instance, I kept in the company for all the months between the idea that I might make the picture until the work began, because I knew she would be an exact "Cameron" girl.

Everyone of the cast proved to be exactly what was required.

When I chose Lillian Gish as Stoneman's daughter, she seemed as ideal for the role as she actually proved herself to be in her acting. Mae Marsh had driven her quality so thoroughly into the estimation of the public in *The Escape* [1914; film made by DWG for Reliance-Majestic/Mutual] that I felt absolutely sure of her results. It was the same with Robert Harron and Elmer Clifton, for Stoneman's sons, and Ralph Lewis as Stoneman lived exactly up to what his personality promised when he was selected. And there were George Siegmann, the mulatto Lieutenant Governor, and Walter Long as the awful Negro Gus, and Mary Alden, Stoneman's mulatto housekeeper.

There has been question as to why I did not pick real Negroes or mulattos for those three roles.

That matter was given consideration, and on careful weighing of every detail concerned, the decision was to have no black blood among the principals; it was only in the legislative scene that Negroes were used, and then only as "extra people."

There were six weeks of rehearsals, before we really began. I think it took something like six months to make the picture—that is, the actual photography; but in all I put in a year and a half of work.

It was a big venture in numbers at that time; I suppose from first to last we used from 30,000 to 35,000 people.

That seemed immense at that era, but now, in the piece we temporarily call *The Mother and The Law* [Mr. Griffith's huge new feature, just completed, and named *Intolerance*], we have used since the first of January about fifteen thousand people a month [this statement was made in the latter part of April 1916], and I cannot see even the beginning of the end as yet.

With *The Clansman* it was not alone the first expense, but the incessant fighting we had to do to keep the picture going, that cost.

We spent over $250,000 the first six months, combatting stupid persecution brought against the picture by ill-minded censors and politicians who were playing for the Negro vote.

Lawyers had to be retained at every place we took the picture, and we paid out enough in rents for theaters where we were not allowed to show the picture to make an average film profitable.

But we finally won.

Now we are showing the picture with no hindrance, and most of those who opposed us at first, are now either admirers of the picture or quiescent.

While on this censorship, this drooling travesty of sense, I want to say something that I have said before, but which is essential to a right understanding of my purposes and work.

The foremost educators of the country have urged upon moving picture producers to put away the slapstick comedies, the ridiculous sentimental "mush" stories, the imitation of the fiction of the cheap magazines and go into the fields of history for our subjects.

They have told us repeatedly that the motion picture can impress upon a people as much of the truth of history in an evening as many months of study will accomplish. As one eminent divine said of pictures, "They teach history by lightning!" [6]

We would like very much to do this, but the very reason for the slapstick and the worst that is in pictures is censorship. Let those who tell us to uplift our art invest money in the production of a historic play of the life of Christ. They will find that this cannot be staged without incurring the wrath of a certain part of our people. "The Massacre of St. Bartholomew," if reproduced, will cut off the toes of another part of our people. [7]

I was considering the production in pictures of the history of the American people. This got into the papers. From all over the country I was strongly advised that this was not the time for a picture on the American Revolution, [8] because the English and their sympathizers would not take kindly to the part the English played in the wars of the American Revolution, and that the pro-Germans would not care to see the Hessians enact their harsh roles in the narrative of our freedom.

Bernard Shaw spoke fatefully and factfully when he said: "The danger of the cinema is not the danger of immorality, but of morality; people, who, like myself, frequent the cinemas testify to their desolating romantic morality. . . ."

If I approach success in what I am trying to do in my coming picture, *Intolerance,* I expect a persecution even greater than that which met *The Birth of a Nation.*

---

[6] A comment attributed to Woodrow Wilson and said to be his reaction to seeing *The Birth of a Nation.*

[7] DWG is, of course, referring here to one of the four stories in *Intolerance.*

[8] DWG's film of the American Revolution was later made as *America* (1924).

The Rise and Fall of Free Speech In America

❖❖❖

WHY CENSOR THE MOTION PICTURE—THE LABORING MAN'S UNIVERSITY?

Fortunes are spent every year in our country in teaching the truths of history, that we may learn from the mistakes of the past a better way for the present and future.

The truths of history today are restricted to the limited few attending our colleges and universities; the motion picture can carry these truths to the entire world, without cost, while at the same time bringing diversion to the masses.

As tolerance would thus be compelled to give way before knowledge and as the deadly monotony of the cheerless existence of millions would be brightened by this new art, two of the chief causes making war possible would be removed. The motion picture is war's greatest antidote.

INTOLERANCE: THE ROOT OF ALL CENSORSHIP

Ours is a government of free speech and a free press.

Intelligent opposition to censorship in the beginning would have nipped the evil in the bud.

But the malignant pygmy has matured into a Caliban.

Muzzle the "Movies" and defeat the educational purpose of this graphic art.

Censorship demands of the picture makers a sugar-coated and false version of life's truths.

The moving picture is simply the pictorial press.

The pictorial press claims the same constitutional freedom as the printed press.

Freedom of speech and publication is guaranteed in the Constitution of the United States, and in the constitution of practically all the states. Unjustifiable speech or publication may be punished, but cannot be

From D. W. Griffith, The Rise and Fall of Free Speech in America (1916), 45-page pamphlet published by DWG. A prefatory note by Griffith states: "This book is not copyrighted. The press is invited to freely use its contents."

forbidden in advance. Mayor Gaynor, that great jurist who stood out from the ordinary gallery-playing, hypocritical type of politician as a white rose stands out from a field of sewer-fed weeds, said in vetoing a moving picture censorship ordinance in the city of New York:

> Ours is a government of free speech and a free press. That is the cornerstone of free government. The phrase "The Press," includes all methods of expression by writing or pictures. . . . If this (moving picture) ordinance be legal, then a similar ordinance in respect to the newspapers and the theaters generally would be legal.

Today the censorship of moving pictures, throughout the entire country, is seriously hampering the growth of the art. Had intelligent opposition to censorship been employed when it first made itself manifest it could easily have been overcome. But the pigmy child of that day has grown to be, not merely a man, but a giant, and I tell you who read this, whether you will or no, he is a giant whose forces of evil are so strong that he threatens that priceless heritage of our nation—freedom of expression.

The right of free speech has cost centuries upon centuries of untold sufferings and agonies; it has cost rivers of blood; it has taken as its toll uncounted fields littered with the carcasses of human beings—all this that there might come to live and survive that wonderful thing, the power of free speech. In our country it has taken some of the best blood of our forefathers. The Revolution itself was a fight in this direction— for the God-given, beautiful idea of free speech.

Afterwards the first assault on the right of free speech, guaranteed by the Constitution, occurred in 1798, when Congress passed the Sedition Law, *which made it a crime for any newspaper or other printed publication to criticize the government.*

Partisan *prosecution of editors and publishers took place at the instance of the party in power,* and popular indignation was aroused against this abridgement of liberty to such an extent that Thomas Jefferson, the candidate of the opposition party for president, was triumphantly elected. And after that nothing more was heard of the Sedition Law, which expired by limitation in 1801.

The integrity of free speech and publication was *not again attacked* seriously in this country until the arrival of the *motion picture,* when this new art was seized by the powers of intolerance as an excuse for an assault on our liberties.

The motion picture is a medium of expression as clean and decent as any mankind has ever discovered. A people that would allow the suppression of this form of speech would unquestionably submit to the suppression of that which we all consider so highly, the printing press.

And yet we find all through the country, among all classes of people, the idea that the motion picture should be censored.

Now, the same reasons which make a censorship of the printed press unconstitutional and intolerable to Americans, make a censorship of the pictorial press unconstitutional and intolerable.

The theory of the constitutional guarantee, in brief, is this: Every American citizen has a constitutional right to publish anything he pleases, either by speech, or in writing, or in print, or in pictures, subject to his personal liability *after publication* to the penalties of violating any law, such as the law forbidding obscenity, libel, and other matter legally unfit for publication.

But the distinction between this theory and a censorship is that a censorship passes upon and forbids printing a picture *before publication,* and so directly controverts the most valuable of all our liberties under the Constitution, which our fathers established for our guidance and our protection.

If the pictorial press can be subjected to censorship by a mere act of Congress, then so can the printed press. And, of course, there would be an end, at once, to the freedom of *writing and printing.*

The constitutional and rightful manner in which to keep the moving pictures within proper bounds is simply to make and to enforce laws which will severely punish those persons who exhibit improper pictures.

As a matter of fact, there are laws now on the statute books which are ample to punish all who deserve punishment. It is simply a question of enforcement. So that the creation of Federal censorship is absolutely unnecessary.

It is said the motion picture tells its story more vividly than any other art. In other words, we are to be blamed for efficiency, for completeness. Is this justice? Is this common sense? We do not think so.

We have no wish to offend with indecencies or obscenities, but we do demand, as a right, the liberty to show the dark side of wrong, that we may illuminate the bright side of virtue—the same liberty that is conceded to the art of the written word—that art to which we owe the Bible and the works of Shakespeare.

Concerning *Intolerance*: Interview with Griffith

◆◆◆

"Is this truly to be your last picture?" Griffith was asked.

"It is," he replied; "Intolerance that I have met with and fought with in my other picture [*The Birth of a Nation*] makes it impossible to ask investment of the tremendous sums of money required for a real feature film with the result dependent on the whim or the lack of brains of a captain of police. . . ."

"You're plucky but you didn't dare finish the picture true to life, and have The Boy executed, as he would have been in real life; Carlyle might well have written your scenario up to that finale, but there you allowed the Despot of the stage to rule and you saved The Boy simply to satisfy the lust for comfort which audiences demand."

"You're one of the fellows who would have stood up and answered Pilate's question, 'What is Truth?'" said Griffith. "That finale *is* Truth, and because it is a comfortable truth you thought it false. If you had read the newspapers as much as you've written for them, you would know about the Stielow case in New York; Stielow was convicted of a murder and sentenced to die; four times he was prepared for the chair, four times he and his family suffered every agony save the final swish of the current. What saved him was exactly what saved The Boy in my picture; the murderer confessed; the final reprieve arrived just as the man was ready to be placed in the chair, his trousers' leg already slit for the electrode."

And picking up the copy of the New York paper containing the account, Griffith read former President Taft's sentence of the criminal law, "The administration of criminal law in this country is a disgrace to civilization. . . ."

"What will you do if *Intolerance* fails?" I asked.

Blandly smiling, he said, "I'll seek the Jersey coast and try to find one of those man-eating sharks."

"And what if it wins?"

Excerpted from Henry Stephen Gordon, "The Real Story of Intolerance,*" Photoplay, X (November, 1916), 34, 37–40. Gordon's article is based on interviews with DWG.*

"I have told you before that this will be my last picture. That is as true as anything can be which the future holds."

"The speaking stage, producing drama?"

"I have told you before that such was my desire; if the picture succeeds it will not, it cannot, make the money that in fabulous fashion pictures are credited with making; theatres cannot hold as much money as some newspapers say some pictures make. The matter of the money to be made is very like the fellow blowing the bassoon in the orchestra who was told to blow louder; 'That's all very well,' he replied, 'but where is the wind to come from?' "

He says he intends to take up the stage next as a means of finding expression unhampered, but when asked what he would do, and how, he side-stepped.

"There will never be any combination of the speaking and the photo drama," he added with a tang of satire, "not if audiences can help it. The stage is perfect now, to my mind, because it enables us to make moving pictures so much easier than it might. I'm sorry that Mansfield, that Daly, that Irving, are dead, but as a moving picture man I am glad, for the movies' sake, that they are gone. If those men were now alive, we of the movies would have to work harder than we do, and I don't know how that could be done, for I figure that now we work fourteen and fifteen hours a day, but if the stage were different we would have to work thirty-six hours in the twenty-four; so we are glad that competition with the stage is not fiercer than it is."

"Don't you regard the modern part of your picture [*Intolerance*] as an attack on the courts, on judges?"

"I certainly do not, because it is not. That Stielow case in New York is exactly like the murder case in the story; only reality goes the picture three better in the way of reprieves. Stielow and his family faced death-suffering four times, and three times the reprieve came at the very last minute. If I had shown scenes like that on the screen it would have made the public laugh as impossible, but the people should not laugh at the courts; judges do not make the laws; you, I, everyone, are responsible for the laws. I have met several judges and have always found them very nice and often very wonderful men. Real gentlemen, in fact. What has seemed peculiar to me about the law is that after so prolonged an experiment with the principles of Christianity we still find as was found through all the ages that justice demands if a man kills another he in turn should be murdered. No, I am far from attacking the courts or judges, for the only thing that has stood between the [moving] pictures and the censors and thereby prevented the pictures from utter extinction, has been the courts. . . .

"The story for Truth as we see it has become barred from the pictures, so that anyone who has a real idea to express should not look to the moving picture as a means, but if he has enough money, to the stage. We of the moving picture craft admit our defeat; it is impossible for us to take any big subject of interest without the fear of the autocrats above us taking away our property. I now contemplate turning to the stage in making an attempt to find freedom of expression."

The New Stage Supplants the Old

◈◇

. . . Already the motion picture is the world's chief form of entertainment, the greatest spiritual force the world has ever known. Here in America it has worked in the course of seven years or so a phenomenal change and it is expanding by leaps and bounds. Already it is the fifth industry in point of riches in America and by all odds the most powerful in point of influence.

Here in America actors, managers, playwrights and producers soon discovered the workings of a tremendous change in the traditional form of entertainment. They watched the end of traveling companies. There are practically none now; those that try the road, save to reach the largest centers, die miserably. Here before me are figures, in fact, that show that last year in twelve months one of many copies of a single film in Illinois and the South played to more people and to more money than all the traveling companies that put out from New York played to in fourteen months. Disregarding the few exceptions, from which I hope something unexpectedly good may come, the old stage is gone, and the new stage is here. It is here, I think, primarily because of the working of economic law, because the man in the small center, and in the large—the typical American, in a word—has discovered that Science offers him something vastly more satisfying, more interesting and more influential for ten cents, or even for five, than the old stage gave at two dollars, or could give at any price at all.

After years of experience on the stage as playwright and actor, I am quite sure not only that the new stage will continue to improve, but

From "Pictures vs. One-Night Stands," Independent, *LXXXVIII* (December 11, 1916), 447–48.

that it has vastly greater potentialities than the old, not only in point of reaching vastly more millions of people but in actual and intrinsic artistic power. For it is clear to me that not only can a producer express any old-stage idea on the new stage at least as effectively as could be done on the old stage, but more effectively. And there are many ideas that I can express, and have exprest [*sic*], with the pictures that could not be exprest [*sic*] on the old stage at all. Within the limitations of the old stage, to illustrate only one phase of the situation, it was impossible to employ more than two plots and difficult enough to have even two. In my *Intolerance* [1916], which I take because it comes first to mind, there are four plots, each in a different century, each in a different part of the world, all drawn together at the end. And I can conceive a play set in one spot, in one stretch of time, with six or seven plots all woven together.

Within the limitations of the old stage it was impossible to employ many technical means that are used with fine effect in the motion pictures. I can accelerate action in a great many ways—by letting two or three stories or plots race along side by side; I can open a play with so simple a thing as a glimpse of a rose, or a glimpse of a beautiful picture; and in a flash I can take the audience from the banks of the Euphrates in Biblical times down to medieval France, or down to the story of a little girl of today.[1]

Acting itself has been improved with this development of the technical means of the play. Many actors have told me that they thought that acting on the old stage was difficult, but that it is nothing compared with acting in the new. . . . Two years ago there was hardly any real actor depending upon the motion pictures. We paid very little attention to the old-stage actors. And when at last we took them and tried them we found they were far beneath in real acting power the ones we had trained. The problem of the old stage and of the new is the same—to permit a playwright to express himself to his audience. The technique is different. The results, I believe, in the new are vastly more effective than in the old, and surely the motion pictures are satisfying millions whom the old stage never satisfied at all. . . .

I know, finally, that because I am a producer of motion pictures, that because I left the old stage for the new, I am likely to be criticized to my own hurt for the conclusions that I have drawn. Yet I have merely tried to make clear that the arts in form are susceptible to a kind of economic and artistic determinism that works ruthlessly to the survival of the fittest.

---

[1] The allusions here are to separate stories in *Intolerance.*

What I Demand of Movie Stars

◈◈◈

I believe that the makers of [moving] pictures have, in many ways, already surpassed the art of the speaking-stage! And perfection in Motion Picture drama has by no means been reached. Far from it, altho [sic] we are advancing with great rapidity. Now, to equal the art of the speaking-stage, a great deal is needed of the people who make these picture-plays, the movie actors and actresses as they are best known. To exceed the art of the speaking-stage, still greater things are needed and demanded of the leaders in the production of a photoplay.

Granted that the person has a moving-camera face—that is, a person who photographs well—the first thing needed is "soul."

"Soul" sounds rather queer in speaking of a movie actor, does it not? Yet, that is just what I mean. The people of the speaking-stage call it temperament, stage presence, technique, and many other things. But there is such a wide difference between the spoken drama and the Motion Picture drama that the big people in the cast of a movie must, in reality, have "soul."

By that I mean people of great personalities, true emotions, and the ability to depict them before the camera. Stage emotions will not do; some of the greatest of actors appear stilted and "stalky" in front of the camera. Every big star in the movies, whether romantic, tragic or comic, really has a most interesting personality. When they step in front of the camera, they do not have the "over-the-footlight" feeling and manner that we see in the actors in the spoken drama. It wouldn't register well at all. When a really good actor stands before the camera, he puts his soul into it—he isn't wondering what the people "down front" are thinking of him. He or she knows there is no audience in front, but a grim, cold-blooded, truth-in-detail-telling camera lens which will register every quiver of the facial muscles, every gleam of the eye, every expression of the face, every gesture, just as it is given.

The movie actor cannot add to his art a soft voice; rising or falling inflection; a deep, piteous sigh; a quickly intaken breath expressing surprise. There can be no gay, rippling laughter, nor solemn tones of

From Moving Picture Classic, *III (February, 1917), 40–41, 68. Footnotes supplied.*

warning; no sad, sweet, pleasant tones; no shrieks of fear—not a sound can help the movie actor. He must express every emotion with his face and hands and with general gestures and movement of the body.

The actor with the soul enters into the work with all the ardor there is in him. He feels his part, he is living his part, and the result is a good picture. I can get quantities of beautiful, doll-faced girls, but, alas! they have no more soul than a doll; they can smile sadly or faintly, or giggle, and that exhausts their capabilities.

For principals I must have people with souls, people who know and feel their parts, and who express every single feeling in the entire gamut of emotion with their muscles!

They do not practice and practice to do that. It comes naturally to them. They practice over and over many stunts, many jumps, dives, and other things, so as to time themselves accurately or so as to learn to do it just right; but when it comes to emotional scenes, whether it is love, hate, joy, sorrow, surprise, chagrin, exultation, or any of the scores of shades of the larger emotions, the best of the actors and actresses just go ahead and do it as tho [sic] it were a part of their really and truly experience in life.

This is but one thing I demand of movie stars. The first thing I demand, of course, is that they have a movie-camera face, and I not only demand that of stars, but of the humblest filler-in. If the person is to appear at all in the picture, that person must be one to photograph well.

A studio picture is quite different from a Moving Picture portrait. A studio picture has every light and shade diffused and thrown here and there so as to accentuate beauty and to hide defects. The negative is then retouched, until the matron of forty comes out on the print like a woman of twenty-five.

We cannot diffuse the light for an interior in the movies, because the people are, naturally, moving. Retouching is out of the question, because one could not retouch a mile or two of film with thousands upon thousands of pictures. Consequently, a director must demand people who take good pictures. Taking a "good" picture does not mean taking a beautiful picture. An old, withered-up woman may take a splendid picture for certain characters. John Bunny[1] did not take a "beautiful" picture, as every one knows, but he certainly took a good picture.

People with very light hair and light blue eyes are seldom successful before the movie camera, because the eyes look white and wild or startled.

---

[1] Celebrated silent film comedian whose portly bulk was often contrasted with his bony costar, Flora Finch.

Good hair, good eyes, good teeth—these are essential for good movie actors, except with character parts. It takes careful search and study to pick out the right people. A graceful carriage is also necessary and the ability to forget the presence of the camera. This prevents restraint, awkwardness and clumsiness, and all those things must be demanded, especially of movie stars.

Somehow, most of the stars who come to us from the regular stage lack sincerity, at least in their earlier efforts before the camera. Mrs. Fiske, in *Tess,* was a notable exception. I know she drew from me the tribute of tears. The Comédie Française actors, notably Coquelin and Le Bargy, who appeared in some of the French pictures, were wonderful in the breadth and strength of their exquisite character portrayals. On the other hand, some of the most widely advertised and most-admired spectacular pictures from abroad suffered from the defect of mediocre acting. Of what use are magnificent scenes with only puppet-like actors? Here in America we are training a school of silent actors who bid fair to surpass the finest efforts of the Old World schools.

In the old days we followed the modes of the stage somewhat slavishly. Few of us sensed we were dealing with a new art form. The primitive picture-play was laid out in acts, strict unity of time and place being always observed, the same-sized figures shown in an unvarying time sequence of single action.

I remember what a sensation I caused in the old Biograph studios, in Fourteenth Street,[2] when I invented the "close-up" figures.

"That will never do at all," objected the proprietors. "The actors look as if they were swimming—you can't have them float on, without legs or bodies!" But I persisted, and had my way, tho [sic] it was alleged that the audiences always knocked disapproval with their feet whenever the "close-ups" were exhibited. Today the "close-up" is essential to every Motion Picture, for the near view of the actors' lineaments conveys intimate thought and emotion that can never be conveyed by the crowded scene.

I borrowed the "cutback" from Charles Dickens. Novelists think nothing of leaving one set of characters in the midst of affairs and going back to deal with earlier events in which another set of characters is involved. I elaborated the "cutback" to the "story within a story" and to the so-called parallel action. I found that the picture could carry, not merely two, but even three or four simultaneous threads of action —all without confusing the spectator. At one point in my latest drama,[3] four actions are represented simultaneously by the device of switching scenes every few moments. Each action heightens the effects

---

[2] The Biograph Company was located at 11 East Fourteenth Street, New York City, when DWG joined that company in 1908.

[3] *Intolerance.*

of the others—a technique that, so far as I am aware, is absolutely novel in story-telling art. My point is that photographic drama is constantly progressing, and he is indeed foolish who would set arbitrary limits as to what it can or cannot accomplish in the course of its marvellous evolution. For one thing, the telling of history, the education of old and young, may be entirely revolutionized by its strangely new processes.

The old schools are coming to us, and appropriating such of our devices as the "cutback" and the parallel action; and I could name one actress, with a tremendous New York hit of two years to her credit, who built up her justly famous part from close study of the methods of our Los Angeles picture actresses!

Already it is admitted that as to poetic beauty the Motion Picture entertainment is far ahead of the stage-play. Poetry is apparently a lost art in the regular theater, but it is the very life and essence of the motion playhouse. We have staged most of Browning's stories, many of Tennyson's innumerable Biblical and classical fables.[4] Not only beauty but thought is our goal, for the silent drama is peculiarly the birthplace of ideas. No one can tell what the Motion Picture will become, for we are at present only at the infancy of it.

I doubt if there ever will be a Shakespeare or Homer of the movies, because the Motion Picture is action, and the fashion of action changes with each age. The stage-work of Forrest, Macready, Kean or Kemble, for example, if it could be accurately reproduced, would appear crude, stiff, awkward to us of today. The acting of today may, similarly, seem unnatural or impossible to the people two hundred years hence. But the immortal stories will be there—the world's legacy of great characters and great scenes—to be picturized according to the changed ideas of the succeeding generations.

I also demand the ability to work, and to work pleasantly and uncomplainingly. It takes endless work to produce a big Motion Picture. Unless the stars are willing to be human and get right into the work, instead of hanging back and acting like superior beings, we cannot produce a really good play.

There is also endless detail. Let me illustrate by the concrete example of *The Birth of a Nation*. First comes the scenario or written outline of the plot. In this case there was a previous stage-play. If we are wise, we forget as much as we can, for the Motion Picture is a novelizing or story-telling form, not strictly a stage form; it is epic rather than dramatic; much of the work is of the great outdoors. We have a period of history to cover, the scenes of a wide territory to revivify. Therefore, we must prepare the locale as well as the actors—

---

[4] Reference to DWG's Biograph film versions of works by Browning and Tennyson.

the tasks of the landscape artist, and in some sense of the civil engineer, are before us. For a month the actors rehearse without the camera.

And now South Carolina, in Reconstruction days, is measurably before our eyes. Elsewhere the battle backgrounds of the Civil War are springing into being, helped by expert advice of old "vets" and modern West Pointers. The costumes, settings and documents are laboriously prepared for the facsimile historical scenes, like those of the Emancipation Proclamation, the Appomattox surrender, and the Lincoln assassination. By the way, twenty-four "Lincoln actors" were rehearsed before the right Lincoln was found! This was because I demand "soul" of the movie star, and for this scene Lincoln was the star part. The Blue and the Gray, the Southern white gentry and the colored contingent all have been drilled under their respective leaders. And then the film-making begins.

At an early stage of the work, after the rough outlines have been filled in, the scenario is thrown away. The building and rebuilding of the story, the piecing of intimate bits and the discarding of the useless go right on while we are living the history, so to speak, from day to day. Nearly twenty-eight miles of pictures—one hundred and forty thousand feet of film—are taken. And how much of these are used? At the finale we discover that we have thrown away eight-tenths of our product; we have remaining twenty-six thousand feet, or, say, five miles of consecutive story. But that is twice too long. At the end of two months more of hard labor we edited *The Birth of a Nation* to twelve thousand or thirteen thousand feet—two hours and forty-five minutes' stage entertainment.

Naturally, a director must demand patience and sincerity as well as "soul" of his movie stars.

Movie Actresses and Movie Acting

❖◈◈❖

The art of acting is at once very simple—and altogether impossible. It isn't what you do with your face or your hands. It's the light within. If you have that light, it doesn't matter much just what you do before

From Harry C. Carr, "How Griffith Picks His Leading Women," Photoplay (December, 1918), pp. 24–26. Interview with DWG.

the camera. If you haven't it—well, then it doesn't matter just what you do, either. Before you give, you must have something to give. This applies to emotions as well as money. . . .

Now, you have asked me about women.

Certainly there are a few mechanical characteristics that have a certain importance. For instance, deep lines on the face of a girl are almost fatal to good screening, for on the screen her face is magnified twenty times, and every wrinkle assumes the proportions of the Panama Canal. It is important that her face have a smooth, soft outline. So with the eyes. Every other physical characteristic is of insignificant importance compared with the eyes. If they are the windows of your soul, your soul must have a window it can see through. The farther motion picture art progresses the more important does this become. In the early days, screen actors put over effects with elaborate and exaggerated gestures. Every year the tendency is more subdued in this regard. Actors make less and less fuss with their hands, and tell more and more with their eyes. But a good pair of eyes and a smooth face of proper contour will not suffice to make a motion picture actress. There are plenty of horses with legs for Derby winners who are pulling milk wagons. They have the legs, but they haven't the fighting heart. In other words, they lack the inward illumination. . . .

Any director can squirt glycerine tears over a pretty face and tip over a few chairs, break up a table or two and have some sort of imitation tragedy. That isn't real. Real tears aren't always real, if you get my meaning. It is the feeling behind the tears that can open the beholder's heart.

Now don't understand me to say that a girl is born a heaven-sent genius or a predestined failure. Nothing could be a more ghastly untruth.

Remember what I said about having something to give, as a preliminary necessity for giving? The only woman with a real future is the woman who can think real thoughts. Some get these thoughts by reading and study; others by instinct. Sometimes deep analytical thought seems to be born in one.

Innovations and Expectations

◆◇◆

. . . A picture is the universal symbol, and a *picture that moves* is a universal language. Moving pictures, someone suggests, "might have saved the situation when the Tower of Babel was built."

The cinema camera is the agent of Democracy. It levels barriers between races and classes.

Visual demonstration is the most impressive means of teaching. Propagandists know this. Educators say that lessons learned with the aid of the moving picture are the least easily forgot. . . .

. . . A dozen years ago "picture acts" became a part of the program of popular vaudeville houses, and at the Eden Musée, in New York, Edison "topicals" were shown. It was about that time [1908] that I began to make film plays at the old Biograph Studio on Fourteenth Street, New York.

In the thirteen years that have passed, I have made five hundred pictures. Some of my early phototales were created under strenuous conditions. When I proposed making a two-reel drama [*Enoch Arden,* 1911], my backers declared that people would never sit through such a long picture. We compromised by cutting the first two-reel picture in half. We named the first part *His Faith,* and the second, *His Faith Fulfilled.* The public liked it and asked for more. Not long afterwards I made a five-reel picture, *The Escape* [1914] and then the first ten-reel drama, *The Birth of a Nation* [1915]. . . .

When I first photographed players at close range, my management and patrons decried a method that showed only the face of the story characters. Today the close-up is employed by nearly all directors to bring a picture audience to an intimate acquaintance with an actor's emotions. When, during the filming of *The Birth of a Nation* [1915], I proposed making a "long shot" of a valley filled with soldiers, I met flat opposition from my staff. Until that time a screen army had numbered half a dozen uniformed men. The rest of the forces were left to the imagination.

I adopted the "flashback" to build up suspense, which till then had

From "Motion Pictures: The Miracle of Modern Photography," The Mentor, *IX, no. 6 (July 1, 1921), 3–12. Footnote supplied.*

been a missing quantity in picture dramas. Instead of showing a continuous view of a girl floating down stream in a barrel, I cut into the film by flashing back to incidents that contributed to the scene and explained it. The photoplay of the present would be counted an arid thing without the diversion supplied by these now familiar aids.

Within late years a daylight screen has been perfected. The combination of the voice and the motion picture has long been an ideal of Mr. Edison and other inventors. I adapted parts of *Dream Street* [1921] to the use of improved "talking pictures." I believe there are great opportunities in the field of the phonograph-projector. Colored photography offers fascinating possibilities. By the use of processes recently patented, subdued natural colors are accurately registered, without the "jumping" that formerly marred the beauty of the tinted picture.

There is a big margin for improvement in the methods of distributing and exhibiting pictures. I hope the time will come when patrons will not be allowed to enter a theater except at the beginning of a photoplay—that the casual hospitality of the picture theater of today will not exist. The public will then regard the performance with the respect they now show for stage plays. This is one phase of the problem that engages us all—how to translate a manufacturing industry into an art, and meet the ideals of cultivated audiences.

For, paraphrasing Walt Whitman, "To have great motion pictures, we must have good audiences, too." [1]

[1] Whitman's actual words were: "To have great poets, there must be great audiences, too" (*Notes Left Over. Ventures, on an Old Theme*).

Youth, the Spirit of the Movies

❖❖

It is youth that wins war. And it is youth that wins audiences. Often, people inquire why movie stars are small in stature and youthful in appearance. Not all of those that are successful are so little—Constance Talmadge, for instance, is not—yet most of the movie heroines are.

Usually, they are little, and they are young. But why?

From Illustrated World (Chicago), *XXXVI (October, 1921), 194–96.*

The answer is that just as all the world loves a lover, so all the world loves youth—youth with its dreams, youth with its eagerness for romance and adventure!

We all love youth. And, after all, few of us, even after we have passed forty, like plays merely as plays. One cannot easily like a play unless in some way it interprets our own lives for us. We have our families, our business, our professions, and we need diversion from our daily problems—that is why nearly twenty millions of us go to a movie every day. Still, we are always interested in youth. If we are past forty, we look back on our youth and think perhaps of things that might have been. And if we are not quite forty, we like to dream with youth of things that still may be. So, either way, we feel the spell of youth.

The older stage did not need in its plays young actors. Yet it needed youth. But, on the older stage, a woman of forty or more could play the part of youth—Sarah Bernhardt plays such parts to this day. But before the camera the woman of forty is—the woman of forty. Truly, the camera is a horrible weapon! On the older stage, with deft makeup and lights dimmed a little, one could play the youthful part, but not before the camera. We have seen them try! On the older stage, we have seen a clever imitator act like a boy or girl, talk like a boy or girl, and look like a boy or girl, and still be forty! But no artist has yet been discovered who can at forty imitate youth successfully before the camera, which exaggerates age amazingly.

So we need youth!

We need youth because the most successful screen stars are not harassed by the technique of the older stage and the requirements of the newer art are very largely different. So a new kind of actor has come to be—the screen actor—just as a new kind of writer is coming to be—the screenwriter. But that isn't all!

It was Victor Hugo, I think, who said you could count on it—a third of your audience will be women, who want beauty and romance and emotion. Nearer two-thirds of all movie audiences, these days, are women. And women are not jealous of little women!

They are, we are told, less jealous of screen heroines than of heroines on the older stage. But they are not at all jealous of little women on the screen! So one producer told a visitor on the lot who inquired why screen heroines are usually so small.

But the real reason is youth!

We pick the little women because the world loves youth, with all its wistful sweetness.

I have found that if actors do not have sweetness inside them, you cannot get it into a photograph of them. No man on earth can bring out what isn't there. And I say this strictly. I think, in illustration, of little Mae Marsh, whom the critics have compared with Duse, even, and Sarah Bernhardt, and mentioned what one of them described as "a kind of aura before her face." On the screen she is always beautiful, and in life as well. She is a wonderful little girl who isn't strong at all, yet she takes care of her mother and is sending her sisters to school. She supports her family.

An audience loves a sweet and kindly face on the screen as in life. The surest guide in the world to lead us out of our daily troubles is a little star who is sweet and gentle and kind, like youth with all its yearnings and simplicity.

For the new drama has the simplicity of youth—it has done away with bombastic, high-falutin' talk.

It is youth, too, that makes the world smile. We laugh at youth— when we are forty—but we smile with it too. And I think we are apt to overestimate a laugh. We laugh all the time—a laugh means little to us.

A laugh is a fine thing in an audience, but it is not so good as a smile—a smile, especially, of the kind that binds pathos and humor together. We laugh at slapstick comedy, but we did not laugh at Joe Jefferson, yet we smiled with him all the time.

In drama, after all, the laugh has its greatest value, probably, as a means of relaxation; but on the screen there are other means, for the whole world is your theater, and relaxation is distinctly a secondary problem.

You can get it in many ways—by accelerating the action, for instance, or by retarding it, by a quick change of scene, by a pause, perhaps a full rest in which you show a little beauty—a rose, close up, perhaps, or green fields, or a baby's hand or foot or winning smile.

But you must have youth—youth with its dreams and sweetness, youth with its romance and adventure! For in the theater, as in our families, we look to youth for beauty and often for example. We sit in the twilight of the theater and in terms of youth, upon faces enlarged, we see thoughts that are personal to us, with the privilege of supplying our own words and messages as they may fit our individual experiences in life.

There we see the truth in silence. Silence, then, becomes more eloquent than all the tongues of men. And the little stars do lead us!

Misplaced Magnificence:
The Bad Taste of Movie Interiors

◆◇◆

Motion pictures have received, and merited, much criticism about the type of rooms they photograph to represent the homes of the rich. Men and women in evening attire depart to the opera or arrive from it. Or a dinner or dance is in progress. Persons of wealth, family and education flash their jewels in the atmosphere of a furniture shop or an auctioneer's showroom. The rooms are crowded with objects that stridently quarrel. I concede the bad taste of such interiors. But there are two reasons that measurably justify the presentation of them. First they are a replica from memory of some drawingrooms. I have seen them as crowded and stifled by ill-assorted and undecorative and conflicting objects in Mayfair. And if a producer had the courage to show a room in a home of wealth that was not crowded with masses of misplaced magnificence he would disappoint his audiences. The producer offers such drawing-rooms and other interiors as the "poorer classes" like to think are the possessions of the rich. If I show a home of refinement as I conceive it to be, where life flows on in smooth beauty, I shall lose money. If occasion offers, however, I shall tempt the lightning of the gods.

From David Wark Griffith, "Are Motion Pictures Destructive of Good Taste?" Arts and Decoration (September, 1923), p. 13.

The Sense of Beauty

◈◈◈

Whatever of truth and beauty is discernible by a generous public in my eager output, I trace to a country boy used to hearing Keats and Tennyson and Shakespeare read at home. The boy of fifteen was a long, "gangling" youth with no slightest claim to beauty for himself. His mother used to address him in kindly admonition. "David," she said, "some people get this world's goods by luck, others by looks and some get it by work. Since you have neither looks nor luck you'll have to get yours by work." The boy did all he could on the farm. One of his duties was to bring four cows home from the pasture every night. As he looks back over the path of retrospect, in the broad beam of varied experience, he concludes that these were the "orneriest" cows that browsed in any pasture of all the world. For when he wanted the cows to walk they would stop, and when he wanted them to stop they would walk. And "night would gather," as the story-writer would say, and the cows, halfway home, would stand gazing at the stars, while the boy shivered at the sound of the wind in the trees. When a branch crackled under feet he was sure the darkness-emphasized sound was made by an Indian or a ghost.

But life was not all stubborn cows and fear-breeding night sounds for that boy. There were hours of sheer beauty. They were evenings spent beside the fireplace when his father, a brigadier-general of the Civil War, whom the neighbors and the men of his company called "Thundering Jake," [1] read from the world's greatest poets and dramatists. Unconsciously I was learning then what consciously now I know, that the root and spring of beauty are in worthy sentiment.

I can summon at any moment a vision of the room in which my father read to my mother, my brother, my sister and me. My sister was a teacher and a not-to-be-despised poet. It was a smallish room with a great fireplace of rough stones. It was part of my day's business to provide the back-log for the fireplace. There were two windows. One

Excerpted from David Wark Griffith, "Are Motion Pictures Destructive of Good Taste?" Arts and Decoration (*September, 1923*), *pp. 12, 13, 79.*

[1] Correctly: "Roaring Jake."

looked upon a wheat field with the turnpike alongside it. The other upon a fringe of black woods. It was a rather bare room, for, like all others of the South, we had little after the war. But the walls were gray. The furniture was dark and old. There were a few good books. That was a beautiful room. Not only for the sentiment of its association but in reality. It possessed the essentials of a room where American life is lived. . . .

I believe that the sense of beauty is developed by environment. If I had children I should try to develop in them the sense of beauty. To do this I should provide them rooms of such simple beauty as the one in which my father's orotund voice poured forth the music of Keats and Tennyson and Shakespeare. Longish rooms, not large, of rather low ceilings and pale gray walls, of dark furniture in graceful lines and of a few forceful pictures—all portraits, among them a portrait of the magnificently ugly face of Abraham Lincoln, a portrait of the gentle philosopher of Concord, Emerson, one of George Washington, the country gentleman, the man who loved the great out-of-doors. There would be a portrait of Robert E. Lee. . . . I should have the portrait of General Grant, sturdy but gentle. . . . There would be one of the old Puritans, too, with their dreams hidden behind stern masks. And in the snow. Roger Williams the builder, rather than Miles Standish the soldier. And Thomas Paine. And a thinker of France: say, Rousseau. Each picture would be an epic. Each would be a well of character inspiration.

Studying One's Audience

◆◇

In one of his earlier successful motion pictures Charles Ray, as a young baseball player whose head had been turned by promotion to the majors, snubs the hometown folks who have come to honor him in the big city.[1] Beside me in the theatre where I watched that film there

From D. W. Griffith as told to Myron M. Stearns, "How Do You Like the Show?" Collier's, April 24, 1926, pp. 8–9. Footnote supplied.

[1] DWG is referring to Thomas Ince's *The Busher,* 1919.

was a pleasant old lady. At the snubbing scene she turned to me—a stranger—and, with voice full of apology as though the youth on the screen were her own son, excused him: "But he's such a *boy!*"

That spontaneous remark, born of sympathy for the boy hero and apology for his shortcomings, was a tribute to the power of the picture. It left no doubt that the film had stirred the woman.

It is not often that you who flock to the movies give us such concrete and striking evidence of your reaction to a screen production. But we who make the movies, who must constantly feel the pulse of the film fans, recognize countless other signs by which you tell us whether the fruits of our efforts bore or please, thrill or amuse. . . .

A great tribute is paid when the unconscious response of an individual in an audience to what he sees reaches a point of actual expression. Sometimes, as when in *The Birth of a Nation,* a black fiend is creeping closer to the tragic little girl of the story, played by Mae Marsh, the call takes the form of a definite warning to an actor on the screen: "Look out!"

At my own studios every single subtitle, every situation, every shift in scene or change in a sequence that is made in editing a film, has to go before an audience for its test before being accepted as part of the completed product. So I have learned to watch audiences closely. . . .

Most motion-picture producers hesitate about going too near the limit of popular approval. Naturally. With so much invested in a single film, it is obvious that only disaster could attend the making of many photoplays that failed to please. And since no one knows exactly what the limit of approval in any particular instance is, the tendency of producers is, of course, to broaden the appeal, even if it means cheapening the character parts and story value of the production.

That is where those of us who make a practice of trying pictures out and studying audiences with almost scientific care have a great advantage. For, since the really great returns are those which come to the photoplays that combine the greatest amount of worthwhile material and leadership with genuine popularity, that knowledge pays big dividends.

We learn, for example, that it is not necessary for a picture to have "everything."

You will respond to a combination of dramatic situation, suspense, excitement, humor and pathos. Or, to any *one* of those things. Laughter and tears are, of course, the two great tributes that are most readily detected. But interest, in the long run, will accomplish wonders at the box office, and the key to interest is suspense. Suspense alone will often carry an entire picture. . . .

When we develop to a still higher point the technique of putting basically fine material across, our progress toward pictures that will please more frequently the intelligent as well as the purely popular element of our ten million patrons a day will be more rapid.

And the more you and your friends, who go to motion pictures because you like them, express your opinions, the better we shall be able to serve you.

Improvement of Acting Standards

❖❖❖

There is a distinct demand from a part of the public for better pictures and better acting, and discriminating people are quick to approve real artistry. I have seen audiences break into applause at a beautiful bit of photography or a fine piece of acting, whereas ten or fifteen years ago they would applaud only when the cavalry arrived in time to save the heroine from the Indians. Unquestionably, standards in acting have improved. More good actors are attracted to the screen today than formerly, when motion pictures were considered beneath the notice of real artists. But we still have our bad actors. Perhaps we shall always have them as long as there are audiences who will accept that kind of performance. What pictures need above everything else is a good story, for without it, even the best acting is unavailable.

From "Don't Blame the Movies!" Motion Pictures Magazine, *XXXI* *(July, 1926), 33, 82. Interview with Griffith.*

Insert Titles: Their Use

❖❖

"Did you know that the first pictures we ever made were without titles?" [Griffith] . . . asked.

From "Don't Blame the Movies!" Motion Picture Magazine, *XXXI* *(July, 1926), 33, 82. Interview with Griffith.*

I shook my head in surprise. *The Last Laugh*[1] was the first picture I had ever heard of without titles and everybody declared it an innovation. Mr. Griffith kept on smiling.

"Yes, we decided that titles—provided they are the right sort, help a picture. Many important feet of film are saved by the simple expedient of using a few printed words," he explained. "Instead of showing a man walking all the way home we found that the action was speeded up and the story made more compact by saying that the man went home. I think in spite of all the fuss that was made about the absence of titles in the German film, it would have been much improved if they had been included. Every foot of film is precious, in telling a story, just as every word in a well-knit drama should have some definite place in the scheme of the play. Ibsen's dramas are constructed like sturdy houses and each of his words is a brick that supports another word or another thought. A play, whether it is on the legitimate stage or on the screen, must have pace. It should not be allowed to lag."

[1] *The Last Laugh (Der Letzte Mann)* directed by F. W. Murnau, Germany, 1925; starred Emil Jannings.

The Greatest Theatrical Force

◆◇◆

Can it be twenty years since motion pictures first sneaked into the theatres, only to stay and become the biggest theatrical force in the world?

The worries then were pretty much the worries now; better stories, finding actors who could be natural and interesting; struggling to put into pantomime effects which your imagination painted. No one ever satisfied with anything.

Everyone wanted more salary then, as they do today. Then it was forty dollars a week; now it is four thousand dollars a week.

When some little novelty of treatment came up, everyone was excited, remarking it as a great step forward in the work. But tricks are never important. To tell a story sincerely, vividly, and simply: that was the big effort then and it is the big effort now.

From Moving Picture World, *LXXXV (March 26, 1927), 408.*

Many useful new tools for the making of pictures have been created since those early perplexities, but the big implement was then and always will be the mind-power to narrate a story in the medium. Technique is only experience, it is not force. No two stories should ever be told alike, but that requires genius and where can you buy that?

The motion picture is an important medium; perhaps the most important. The people who pride themselves upon their culture and education spurned it in the beginning, for that is the conservative class, always bucking everything new. Kings who were illiterate made reading and writing unpopular in their day.

But pictures have now snipped all croakers aside. And now that the form is somewhat stable, this mighty force is claiming the authority and dominance due it.

Films I Should Like to Make

Pictures are the only medium that can carry big stories, epochal poetry and events—that is what I should like to see, but who knows! If I had my way, I should do Homer's *Iliad, Antony and Cleopatra, The Life of Napoleon, Medea*—things that can never be done as effectively on the speaking stage, stories in which all the illusion of a spectacle and authenticity might be introduced. . . .

Our best screen work will be done through comedy. In comedy, satire, people will accept truth more than in tragedy. Everyone in the world lies or cheats or steals some time in his life. There are few of us who haven't done things we should not have done. In comedy we can exhibit these shortcomings and have the audience enjoy it. In drama the audience does not tolerate that. It demands the conventional virtues. . . .

Most motion pictures are adapted from stage plays and books. The ways of expression used in pictures are different from plays and books. People think in words. It will be a long time before people will think in terms of pictures. Ideas are all right for stage people, but pictures prefer simple, straight stories of facts.

From "The Motion Picture Today—and Tomorrow," Theatre, XL (October, 1927), 21, 58.

Tomorrow's Motion Picture

❖❖❖❖❖❖❖❖❖❖❖❖❖❖❖❖❖❖❖❖❖❖❖❖❖❖❖❖❖❖❖❖❖❖❖❖❖❖❖

What of tomorrow and the motion picture industry? Will the ugly duckling indeed become a swan? Will the overgrown Infant and awkward Child become a fleet-winged Youth, aflame with grace and beauty? The fond parents and the hosts of godfathers and mothers say "Yes."

There is a thought that I would stress right here—a thought all too frequently forgotten or overlooked, which is—that motion pictures are really a *new* form of literary and artistic expression. This fact was recognized in the beginning, in the days of the one-reel and split-reel subject; later on, it seemed to be lost sight of entirely.

When motion pictures were first seriously admitted to be a medium for presenting a coherent story they were written directly for the screen —and *idea* was all that was necessary. I recall the advertisement of one of the innumerable "scenario schools" which declared that all the writer ambitious for screen honors required was an "idea on a cuff." Quickly the day came when a *story* was demanded; this was the day of the daringly inflated "two-reeler"; after which, with bewildering rapidity came three, four and five reel "features," with room for character development and "comedy relief."

Next came the time when popular stories, plays and novels were in demand for "screen material." Every studio kept a staff to read old, out-of-copyright books and magazines; the classics were brought up to date, or made into "historical dramas"; new books and plays were bought at good prices—an era of foolish buying resulted, for a "best-seller" does not always make a good story for the screen.

Which brings me to a thought which may have important bearing on the motion picture of tomorrow. It is my belief that certain writers are supreme in the short-story craft. O. Henry and Kipling come at once to mind as examples of this medium at its best; that other writers require the detail of the novel in order to fully illustrate their talent, and the names of Dickens, H. G. Wells, and Conrad prove my point; Shakespeare belongs on the stage; and what of the screen? Must it be the step-child of literature, forever wearing remodelled garments, cut down and clumsily refilled from another member of the same family?

I do not believe the motion picture will ever achieve real greatness

From The Picturegoer (*London; June, 1928*), p. 11.

until it can boast its own O. Henry, Dickens, or Shakespeare; and I further believe the day is not so far away as many imagine when screenwriting will be specialised. To this end I hope soon to hear of rigid tests for those who aspire to become writers for the screen. There are, I know, several colleges now teaching screenwriting. This is a step in the right direction; but too often, entrance is effected through literary ability. This is not enough; the applicant for screenwriting must have a screen mind; he must be able to visualize clearly and consecutively.

Whereas the novelist must have the power of description, of character delineation, combined with all the other elements of plot, counterplot, and so on, and the short-story writer must have the technique of his difficult craft at his fingertips, making five words of trenchant meaning cover the novelist's chapter, just so must the screenwriter be trained in the medium he chooses; not for the scenarist the wayside loitering and daffodil plucking accorded the leisurely novelist. It is the screenwriter's business to follow a sharply defined trail.

When he writes "Scene 1," he must mentally see it reaching out in unbroken continuity to Finis. If a flawless continuity, correct in detail as a blueprint, is handed the director, then may the latter pluck or plant his own blossoms along the way; interpretation of a creation— the director playing Paderewski to the screenwriter's Beethoven.

Another encouraging indication that the motion-picture industry is striving to effect beneficial results within itself is the reception again being accorded original stories.

The plagiarism (as often as not unintentional—but when intentional so far-reaching in its disastrous results that it gave a very black eye to honest writers) before mentioned was perhaps the immediate factor in closing the doors to ambitious screenwriters; another factor was poor stories.

But having spent millions of dollars for the screen rights to novels, stories and plays that were found, when stripped of their verbiage, to be just familiar old plot-skeletons, the astute producers have turned over the doormat, again exposing the WELCOME sign, and discouraged screenwriters are dusting their typewriter keys.

Another hopeful sign for tomorrow's motion picture is a recognition that a photoplay may indeed be worthy of the name and classification of "literature," which we see illustrated in the better pictures that are being shown on the screen today; whereas, yesterday's picture depended almost entirely on *plot,* the better pictures of today are triumphs of characterization.

A few years ago the whimsies of a Barrie might have been denied their place on the screen but every day brings us closer to that tomorrow wherein the screen shall come into its own as a powerful and novel form of literature.

ESSAYS

Realism and Romance:
D. W. Griffith
by A. NICHOLAS VARDAC

[Griffith's] first release, *The Adventures of Dollie* (Biograph, July 14, 1908), borrowed a melodramatic subject previously treated by [Edwin S.] Porter in *Stolen by Gypsies* [1905] and used a similar editorial structure. It was an outdoor film, hence pictorially realistic. To this realism Griffith added his own romantic touch. In the Porter film, Dollie had been accidentally found and recognized by her former nurse years after her kidnaping, and then simply rescued from the gypsies by the police. But in the Griffith picture, the gypsies hid her

in a water cask, put it on their wagon and sped away. As they pass over a stream, the cask falls off the wagon and into the water where it is carried by a strong current downstream, over a waterfall, through secthing rapids, finally to enter the quiet cove of the first scene. Fishing boys hearing strange sounds from the cask break it open and discover Dolly [sic]. Soon she is safe in the arms of her overjoyed papa and mama.[1]

To the hard-edged melodrama of Porter, Griffith began by adding a fuller pictorial development, both sentimental and romantic.

With such romantic material he began to refine Porter's editorial approach with techniques directed toward a more thorough realism. In his filming of *For Love of Gold* [1908], from Jack London's romantic melodrama, *Just Meat,* he made progress in the realistic presentation of character. Previous to this, the usual method for revealing the men-

Reprinted by permission of the publishers from A. Nicholas Vardac, Stage to Screen *(Cambridge, Mass.: Harvard University Press), pp. 200–10. Copyright 1949 by the President and Fellows of Harvard College.*

[1] *Biograph Catalogue*, Bulletin 151 (July 14, 1908), film 3454.

tal reaction of a character had been with a double-exposure "dream balloon" flashed above his head. Griffith eliminated this conventional technique by cutting down the editorial unit from a full scene "take" to a single "shot." The climactic scene in this picture, showing two thieves dividing their latest plunder, developed out of the fear of each that the other suspected a double-cross. Suspense and drama arose over which would first succeed in getting rid of the other, and how. This was, in its small way, the beginning of a long line of psychological thrillers, since the thieves managed to poison each other's coffee. Dramatic climax was developed through the use of a single "shot" within the scene "take." Instead of playing the entire scene before a stationary camera, with action proceeding as if on a stage, both actors visible at once, and with "dream balloons" coming to the aid of their pantomime, Griffith shifted his camera to shoot one or the other as the dramatic focus demanded. Where whole scenes had been the previous editorial unit, single shots were used here. The result was greater realism in the presentation of character and a more fluid cinematic continuity.

This use of the single shot as editorial unit had a still further effect. By eliminating all distractive elements at the moment when the reaction of the individual character became the significant dramatic value, it reduced the necessity for exaggerated acting and overplaying. Restraint in acting, hence greater realism of character, became possible.

With this start toward a more realistic treatment of character and toward a smoother and more articulate editorial pattern, Griffith sought next to improve the realism of the photography itself through an aesthetic approach to lighting. In *Edgar Allan Poe* (Biograph, 1909), he achieved a three-dimensional quality, therefore greater realism in photography, with the use of light and shade. It is of interest, too, that this new photographic realism was again coupled with a subject straight from the heart of nineteenth-century romance, dealing, as it did, with Poe's *The Raven* and incidents in the poet's baroque and abnormal life. The need for this realism in photography led Griffith into further successful experiments with lighting. In *A Drunkard's Reformation* (Biograph, 1909), he photographed fire burning in a fireplace in a darkened room. The weird, grotesque effect, with its ephemeral shadows and fugitive figures, created a startling and realistic illusion on the screen. In *Pippa Passes* (Biograph, 1909), he discarded the usual editorial form of melodrama and in a simple, direct story leaned heavily upon the pictorial appeal of his realistic lighting. Morning, Noon, Evening, and Night, the four parts of the film, were realistically filmed. And while Browning was the most rarefied dramatic stuff up to date, it was reported that "the adventurous producers who inaugurated these expensive departures from cheap melodrama are being overwhelmed by offers from renting agents." [2] The appeal of simple pictures realistically presented by means of the new developments in film lighting equaled the box-office draw of melodrama.

This advance in realistic photography was followed by further progress in the articulation of motion-picture syntax and in realistic character portrayal. A one-reel version of *Enoch Arden*, rechristened *After Many Years* (Biograph, 1908), sacrificed both melodramatic structure and the usual chase sequence. Much of its success came out of the editorial technique. It was the first film to use the "close-up" to reveal more realistically than could the full shot what was going on in the minds of the characters. The visualization of a state of mind arose out of the manner in which the close-up was worked into the fabric of the film. For instance, from a close-up of Annie brooding in her seaside cottage over the fate of her long-departed Enoch the camera dissolves to a shot of Enoch shipwrecked on the desert island. The juxtaposition of these two strips of film suggested to the spectator a psychic relationship between the two which, with its reduction of spatial limitations, was not only a marvel of pictorial realism but marked the beginnings of subjective revelation of character in the cinema.

The Lonely Villa (Biograph, 1909) indicated further advance in the realism of the pictorial medium with a cross-cutting technique which left little to the imagination of the audience. A husband leaves wife and children alone in their remote villa to drive twenty miles away to fetch his mother. Robbers break into the villa. The husband's car breaks down. He calls his wife on the telephone just in time to hear her terrified cries before the wires are cut. Between these parallel lines of action a cross-cutting technique, new in its rapidity and dynamic development, was employed. Both lines of action were transferred to the screen exactly as they were progressing. The visual impact of the rapid-fire succession of "takes" developed a dynamic crescendo of suspense which was relieved only at the breaking point by the husband's last-minute arrival to effect a rescue. This cross-cutting technique was repeated in *The Lonedale Operator* (Biograph, 1911), heightening the melodramatic values through facile and realistic pictorial presentation and thus perfecting the technique employed many years before in the melodrama of the stage.

Griffith worked continually to increase graphic realism. It seems that every refinement in editorial technique was associated with this desire. In *Ramona* (Biograph, 1910), he combined the long shot with the full shot and the close-up. This of itself marked progress toward a fluid cinematic structure. But at the same time the underlying significance of this development is that each type of shot was devoted to that special

[2] *The New York Times,* October 10, 1909.

purpose which seemed "right" or real in view of the dramatic value of the particular scene being filmed. The vantage point of the camera was changed in the same way that an ideal spectator, wishing to gain a real view of the action without being distracted, would change his position. The technique of photography joins here with that of editing to cast off elements of conventionality and to attain a truer realism. Action was now shown as an ideal spectator would wish to see it had he actually been present.

With the use of the full shot, more restrained acting had become possible than in the early filming of a full scene before a static camera. Similarly, the close-up allowed for more realistic acting than did the full shot. In *The New York Hat* (Biograph, 1912), this refinement in the articulation of the camera made possible a break away from the broad, stereotyped, robust, and artificial pantomime of the earlier films.

Griffith ever sought new methods and fresh areas. The Biograph Company, on the other hand, was more conservative. Experiments, innovations, and improvements were welcomed as long as they were successful and as long as they remained in the areas of editorial technique and camera articulation, for here no productional investment was necessary. Longer films, with costly production, were as yet unproved and here Biograph opposed the genius of Griffith. He succeeded, despite opposition from the company officials, in refilming *Enoch Arden* in two reels in 1911. He defied the policy of Biograph in this case on the basis of a film which relied as much on the spectacle appeal of California backgrounds as upon the popularity of a well-known stage subject.

It was becoming increasingly difficult to add new and more realistic refinements to the editorial structure established by Porter. Griffith began to look in new directions. Editorial and photographic advancements had been achieved; productional expansion appeared to be the next logical step. His first attempt at a longer film had been stymied by the conservative Biograph policy, which forced a single-reel release of the two-reel version of *Enoch Arden*. Consequently, his next attempt at a spectacle film, *The Battle* (Biograph, 1911), retained the single-reel form but involved a larger pictorial conception, employing hundreds of soldiers fighting in trenches, on the run, on the march, suggesting what was later to be fully developed in *The Birth of a Nation*. Large-scale spectacle became a part of the fabric of the melodramatic photoplay.

The psychology of a bevy of village lovers is conveyed in a lively sweethearting dance. Then the boy and his comrades go forth to war. The lines pass between hand-waving crowds of friends from the entire neighborhood. These friends give the sense of patriotism in mass. Then as the consequence of this feeling, as the special agents to express it, the soldiers are in battle. By the fortunes of war the onset is unexpectedly near to the house where once was the dance.

The boy is at first a coward. He enters the old familiar door. He appeals to the girl to hide him, and for the time breaks her heart. He goes forth a fugitive not only from battle, but from her terrible girlish anger. But later he rallies. He brings a train of powder wagons through fires built in his path by the enemy's scouts. He loses every one of his men, and all but the last wagon, which he drives himself. His return with that ammunition saves the hard-fought day.

And through all this, glimpses of the battle are given with a splendor that only Griffith has attained.[3]

This combination of spectacle and melodrama was so successful, and the treatment in this short picture so popular, that even after the feature-length film had been established, *The Battle* was reissued June 11, 1915, four years after its original production.

In 1912 the second significant American spectacle film and the first to recognize the challenge of current European spectacles was produced. This was Griffith's *The Massacre* (Biograph, 1912). Again the enlargement of the scope of film melodrama was attained through the addition of spectacle. Again a romanticized historical subject was reproduced with realism. Custer's last stand came to life. On the West Coast, far from the dingy offices of Eastern film magnates, cries for budget reduction fell unheard. Hundreds of cavalrymen and scores upon scores of Indians were unleashed. Costumes and sets reached a new high for lavishness in American films. But the release came too late, for new European spectacles of a more magnificent scale had already reached American exhibitors and Griffith's *The Massacre* passed unnoticed in the crowd.

Within the single-reel form Griffith had aimed, first of all, at heightening the realism of the camera, of acting, and of the production; secondly, toward a refinement and articulation of the melodramatic cinematic syntax originally demonstrated by Porter; and thirdly, at an enlargement of the pictorial and productional conception of the film through the addition of spectacle. Throughout the last years of this single-reel development, the influence of the foreign film was being felt and it must have reached Griffith, for, either under its stimulus or in his own creative spontaneity, he had begun to offer a certain compe-

[3] Vachel Lindsay, *The Art of the Moving Picture* (New York: Macmillan, 1915), pp. 43–44.

tition to European importations. A steadily increasing stream of historical spectacles shows an early recognition of the cinematic possibilities of this form. *The Slave* (Biograph, 1909) was a melodrama set in Roman times, supported by "a series of most beautiful pictures of the Romanesque type." [4] In the following week came *The Mended Lute*, with a great deal of authentic spectacle

> based on the life and customs of the American aboriginals. . . . Much thought and time were given the many details, and we may claim that as to costumes, manners and modes of living, it is more than reasonably accurate, these details having been supervised by an expert. . . . The subject as a whole is a combination of poetical romance and dramatic intensity, the canoe chase being the most picturesque and thrilling ever shown.[5]

The addition of historical spectacle to melodrama was consciously taking place in a large body of the Biograph output. *The Death Disc* (1909) exploited historical costumes of the Cromwellian period; *The Call to Arms* (1910) was a story of the Middle Ages with picturesque period paraphernalia and background; *Wilful Peggy*, of the early days in Ireland; *The Oath and the Man*, of the French Revolution; *Rose o' Salem Town*, of Puritan witchcraft; *Heartbeats of Long Ago*, of fourteenth-century Italy; *The Spanish Gypsies*, of sunny Andalusia, and so on. A full series of Spanish and Mexican films was produced. Browning's *A Blot on the 'Scutcheon* was produced with complete costumes in 1912. *Lena and the Geese* (1912) went to old Holland for its locale. Two reels were devoted to *A Pueblo Legend* (1912), authentically spectacular and filmed on location in Old Pueblo of Isleta, New Mexico. Costume plates and shields, weapons and accessories were loaned by the Museum of Indian Antiques at Albuquerque.[6] The success of these authentic historical spectacles on the screen demonstrates the continuation by the film of the approach and the manner of the nineteenth-century stage.

Griffith's romanticism was as evident in his choice of players as in his subject matter. Lewis Jacobs has observed that "all his heroines—Mary Pickford, Mae Marsh, Lillian Gish, Blanche Sweet—were, at least in Griffith's eye, the pale, helpless, delicate, slim-bodied heroines of the nineteenth century English poets." [7] It was this same romantic bias which, when added to the stimulus supplied by the success of

---

[4] *Biograph Catalogue*, Bulletin 261 (July 29, 1909), film 3598.

[5] Ibid., Bulletin 263 (August 5, 1909), film 3601.

[6] Ibid., Bulletin (August 29, 1912), film 3994.

[7] Jacobs, *The Rise of the American Film*, p. 97.

lavish European spectacles, suggested the subject for an early attempt at supremacy in the field of the spectacle film.

Working in comparative secrecy in the town of Chatsworth, far from the Los Angeles film colony, Griffith began production in 1912 of a Biblical spectacle. In the following year he completed *Judith of Bethulia*, the first American four-reel film designed for feature-length exhibition. The picture was not released until 1914, and in the interim Griffith's association with Biograph had terminated. His reckless extravagance in this production led the company to request his resignation as director. The balm of appointment as producer-adviser in the productions of newer directors was insufficient to prevent his complete separation from Biograph and his immediate entrance into the Majestic-Reliance Company.

Judith of Bethulia borrowed its material from the scriptural spectacle of the same name by Thomas Bailey Aldrich, currently successful upon the stage. Needless to say, the stage production, impeded by physical limitations, was dwarfed by Griffith's screen version. An entire army of Assyrians, authentically garbed and marshaled in the manner of the period, was thrown against the city walls. The production involved feats of engineering.

> Between two mountains was the location chosen for the great wall against which Holofernes hurls his cohorts in vain attacks. Eighteen hundred feet long, and broad enough to permit of the defenders being massed upon it, the wall rose slowly until it was a giant's causeway connecting the crags on either side. Within, a city sprang up, in whose streets take place some of the most thrilling scenes in the picture. Beyond it, in the valley, was pitched the great armed camp of the Assyrians. In the chieftains' tent alone were hangings and rugs costing thousands of dollars.[8]

This was the most expensive production Biograph had yet attempted. Great numbers, more than one thousand people and about three hundred horsemen, were marshaled. The monstrous scale of the conception did not interfere with the development of details and authentic properties.

> The following were built expressly for the production: a replica of the ancient city of Bethulia; a faithful reproduction of the ancient army camps embodying all their barbaric dances; chariots, battering rams, scaling ladders, archer towers, and other special war paraphernalia of the period.

[8] *The Biograph Weekly*, I, no. 2 (New York: September 12, 1914), 11.

The following spectacular effects: the storming of the walls of the city of Bethulia; the hand-to-hand conflicts; the death-defying chariot charges at breakneck speed; the rearing and plunging horses infuriated by the din of battle; the wonderful camp of the terrible Holofernes, equipped with rugs from the Far East; the dancing girls in their exhibition of the exquisite and peculiar dances of the period, the routing of the command of the terrible Holofernes, and the destruction of the camp by fire.[9]

Vachel Lindsay, in his excellent description of this film, has pointed out that the structure of this spectacle employed an editorial form utilizing four sorts of scenes. There were scenes showing (1) the particular history of Judith and Holofernes; (2) the wooing of Naomi by Nathan; (3) the streets of Bethulia massed with the people in their sluggish mass movement; and finally, (4) scenes of the assault, with camp and battle scenes interpolated, to unify the continuity.[10] Spectacle had, at the cost of $32,000,[11] assumed the salient position and melodrama existed only as a means for exploiting spectacle. And it was through editorial patterns demonstrated in the melodrama that the preceding four types of scenes were integrated. The story of Judith and Holofernes and the courtship of Nathan and Naomi were subsidiary to the spectacle and derived their dramatic stature and significance from the spectacle. Nathan and Naomi, for instance, "are seen among the reapers outside the city or at the well near the wall, or on the streets of the ancient town. They are generally doing the things the crowd behind them is doing, meanwhile evolving their own little heart affair." [12] This heart affair of two black and white figures flickering across the screen gained its dramatic power through editorial association with the huge, spectacular environment and with the masses whose mob mind could be visually dramatized upon the screen. Naomi and Nathan transcended the personality of mortals. Their own little personal drama, woven into the vast tapestry of the spectacle, gained thereby an emotional significance which far exceeded the possibilities of simple chase melodrama. The limitations of conventionalized character portrayal were removed by an editorial pattern involving elements of spectacle. When Naomi is rescued by her sweetheart, Nathan, this "act is taken by the audience as a type of the setting free of all the captives." [13] Judith similarly derives her stature from Bethulia, and

[9] From a contemporary review (unidentified), quoted in Lindsay, *The Art of the Moving Picture*, p. 59.
[10] Lindsay, *The Art of the Moving Picture*, p. 60.
[11] Linda Arvidson (Mrs. D. W. Griffith), *When the Movies Were Young*, p. 225.
[12] Lindsay, *The Art of the Moving Picture*, p .62.
[13] Ibid., p. 64.

Holofernes achieves his dramatic identity as the personification of the Assyrian army. Thus, through a clever editorial form, the dramatic as well as the pictorial scale of the cinema was extended. Spectacle values had become absolutely necessary to the development of the silent motion picture. And it was a recognition of these values that had prompted Griffith's entrance into the feature film with *Judith of Bethulia*.

With the arrival of the feature film came improvement in the use of musical accompaniment. Stage melodrama and early screen melodrama had, of course, both used musical accompaniment to the action. It had been stereotyped, direct, and bold in its intention, oftentimes the impromptu creation of the pianist or organist bred to the work. For *Judith*, however, a complete musical accompaniment with specific predetermined cues was provided.

> Open with *Maritana* (Wallace) until Judith in Prayer:
> Then *The Rosary* (Nevin) until she leaves woman with child:
> Then *Maritana* until "The Army":
> Then *William Tell* (Rossini) the last movement. Play this to end of reel:
> Then *Pique Dame*, overture (Suppe) all through:
> Then *Poet and Peasant*, overture (Suppe) until "Water and Food Famine":
> Then *Simple Aveu* (Thome) until "The King":
> Then *Peer Gynt*—Suite II, opus 55 (Grieg) until Judith has vision:
> Then *Woodland Sketches I & II* (MacDowell) until she dons fine clothes:
> Then *Lament of Roses* (Sonnakolb) until "The King":
> Then *Peer Gynt*—Suite II, opus 55 (Grieg) until end of reel.[14]

Music, an integral part of nineteenth-century melodrama and spectacle, was utilized here by the screen in the same fashion. The quality of the music, obviously enough, was calculated in its naïve way to heighten the intensity of the scene.

Through the work of D. W. Griffith in the period from 1908 to 1913, motion pictures progressed from single-reel storyettes and topical episodes to successful experiment with the feature-length spectacle film. Griffith had come to the films with a rich background of Victorian romanticism both in the theatre and in his general approach to life. Without sacrificing any of his strong romantic bias, he developed the realistic capacities of this medium to serve in the exploitation of his

[14] Clarence E. Sinn, "Music for Pictures," *Moving Picture World*, XX, no. 1. (April 4, 1914), 50.

romantic conceptions. Whatever progress Griffith made in the development of a cinematic syntax had always been motivated by his quest for a greater and more fluid screen realism, whether for character portrayal, scenic production, or narrative development. In this way, he pioneered in the evolution of a technique for this new art form, which was originally derived from the forms of the nineteenth-century stage but which succeeded in eliminating the restrictions and conventions with which this stage had been fettered.

In the search for greater realism Griffith carried this editorial development to a point beyond which improvement was difficult. And at about this time the influence of foreign spectacle films was being felt in this country. Responding to these two coincidental conditions, Griffith made his first attempt at a feature-length film on the basis of a spectacular production with *Judith of Bethulia*. He took his material directly from the stage and surpassed the stage in its production. In this way, presenting a romanticized historical spectacle in an authentic and lavish fashion within the melodramatic cinematic structure, Griffith produced the first American four-reel photoplay. He appears, then, as the strongest and most successful of the early screen continuators of nineteenth-century melodrama and spectacle, of realism and romance.

How Griffith Came to Make

THE BIRTH OF A NATION

by LINDA ARVIDSON

Now before the Kinemacolor Company had started work at White-stone[1] they had held a contract with George H. Brennan and Tom Dixon for the production in color of Tom Dixon's *The Clansman*. The idea was that the dramatic company touring through the Southern states in *The Clansman* would play their same parts before the camera. In these Southern towns all the Southern atmosphere would be free for the asking. Houses, streets, even cotton plantations would not be too remote to use in the picture. And there was a marvelous scheme for interiors. That was to drag the "drops" and "props" and the pretty parlor furniture out into the open, where with the assistance of some sort of floor and God's sunshine, there would be nothing to hinder work on the picture version of the play.

But the marvelous scheme didn't work as well as was expected; and eventually the managers decided that trying to take a movie on a fly-by-night tour of a theatrical company was not possible, so the company laid off to take it properly. They halted for six weeks and notwithstanding the sum of twenty-five thousand dollars was spent, it was a poor picture and was never even put together. Although Tom Dixon's sensational story of the South turned out such a botch, it was to lead to a very big thing in the near future.

Frank Woods, after several others had tried, had written the continuity of this version of *The Clansman*, and had received all of two hundred dollars for the job. That the picturizing of his scenario had

From Linda Arvidson, When the Movies Were Young *(New York: Dutton, 1925), Chapter XXVIII, pp. 249–55. Footnotes supplied.*

[1] The Kinemacolor Company of America proceeded in the summer of 1912 to establish a studio in Whitestone, Long Island, for the purpose of making color movies.

proved such a flivver did not lessen his faith in *The Clansman's* possibilities.

Mr. Griffith was doing some tall thinking. His day of one- and two-reelers having passed, and the multiple-reel Mutual features[2] having met with such success, he felt it was about time he started something new. So, one day, he said to Frank Woods: "I want to make a big picture. What'll I make?" With his Kinemacolor experience still fresh in mind Mr. Woods suggested *The Clansman.* With the Dixon story and the play Mr. Griffith was quite familiar as he had heard from his friend Austin Webb, who had played the part of the mulatto *Silas Lynch,* about all the exciting times attending the performance of the play—the riots and all—and more he had heard from Claire Mac-Dowell, who was also in the show, and more still from Mr. Dixon himself.

So David Griffith said to Frank Woods: "I think there's something to that. Now you call Mr. Dixon up, make an appointment to see him, and you talk it over, but say nothing about my being the same actor who worked for him once."

So the meeting was arranged; the hour of the appointment approached; and as Mr. Woods was leaving on his important mission Mr. Griffith gave final parting instructions, "Now remember, don't mention I'm the actor that once worked for him, for he would not have confidence in me."

So while Tom Dixon nibbled his lunch of crackers, nuts, and milk, Mr. Woods, without revealing his little secret, unfolded the mighty plan, "We are going to sell Wall Street and get the biggest man in the business."

"Who?"

"D. W. Griffith."

"Oh, yes, I've heard a lot about him—he used to work for me."

Mr. Dixon was greatly interested and evinced no hesitation whatever in entrusting his sensational story of the South to his one-time seventy-five dollars a week actor. He'd already taken one sporting chance on it, why not another? Yes, Mr. Griffith could have his *Clansman* for his big picture.

H. E. Aitken, who had formed the Mutual Film Company, had had on his Executive Committee Felix Kahn, brother of Otto Kahn, and Crawford Livingston. They had built the Rialto and Rivoli Theatres. The Herculean task of financing the "big picture," Mr. Aitken presented to Mr. Kahn, and he genially had agreed to provide the necessary cash—the monetary end was all beautifully settled—when the

[2] After leaving the Biograph Company in 1913, DWG joined the Reliance-Majestic Company, for which he made four multi-reel films that were distributed through the Mutual Film Corporation.

World War entered the arena and Mr. Kahn felt he could not go on. So Mr. Aitken had to finance the picture himself. He financed it to the extent of sixty thousand dollars, which was what *The Birth of a Nation* cost to produce. With legal fees and exploitation, it came to all of one hundred and ten thousand dollars. Mr. Felix Kahn and Mr. Crawford Livingston afterwards offered to help out with fifteen thousand dollars but there were fifteen directors on the executive committee of the Mutual Film, and they overruled the fifteen thousand dollars tender, leaving Mr. Aitken as sole financier.

Mr. Dixon received two thousand five hundred dollars cash and 25 percent of the profits. He wanted more cash—wasn't so interested in the profits just then. But afterwards he had no regrets. For it happened sometimes in later days, when the picture had started out to gather in its millions, that Mr. Dixon casually opening a drawer in his desk, would be greeted by a whopping big check—his interest in *The Birth of a Nation,* and one of these times, happening unexpectedly on one such check, he said, "I'm ashamed to take it"—a sentiment that should have done his soul good.

Well, Mr. Dixon is one who should have got rich on *The Birth of a Nation,* but the one whose genius was responsible for the unparalleled success of the epoch-making picture says he fared like most inventors and didn't get so rich. However, it probably didn't make Mr. Griffith so very unhappy, for so far he has seemingly got more satisfaction out of the art of picture-making than out of the dollars the pictures bring.

Had the Epoch Company not sold State Rights on the picture when they did, Tom Dixon's interest would have been fabulous. But as the State Rights' privilege was not for life, only for a term of years, now soon expiring, or perhaps expired now, and as up to date the picture has brought in fifteen million dollars, it seems as though there's nothing much to be unhappy about for any of those concerned.

One of the State Rights buyers who took a sporting chance on the picture was Louis B. Mayer, who had begun his movie career with a nickelodeon in some place like East or South Boston,[3] borrowing his chairs from an undertaker when they weren't being used for a funeral. Mr. Mayer managed to scrape together enough money to buy the State Rights for New England and he cleaned up a small fortune on the deal after the owners had figured they had skimmed all the cream off Boston and other New England cities. . . .

And so eventually *The Birth of a Nation* was finished. At the Liberty Theatre in West Forty-second Street, New York—1915 was the time—

[3] Louis B. Mayer's American Feature Film Company was established in Boston. In 1915 Mayer became secretary of the newly established Metro Pictures Corporation. See further Chapter V of Bosley Crowther's *The Lion's Share* (New York: Dutton, 1957).

it had its première—one wholly novel for a moving picture—for it was the first time a movie was presented bedecked in the same fashion as the more luxurious drama, and shown at two dollars per seat. It was not the first picture to be given in a legitimate theatre, however, for Mr. Aitken had previously booked at the Cort Theatre *The Escape*,[4] the picture made from the Paul Armstrong play of the same name. At this first public projection of *The Birth of a Nation*,[5] an audience sat spellbound for three hours. The picture was pronounced the sensation of the season. From critics, ministers, and historians came a flood of testimonials, treatises, and letters on the new art and artists of the cinema.

The Birth of a Nation remains unique in picture production. It probably never will be laid absolutely to rest, as it pictures so dramatically the greatest tragedy in the history of America, showing the stuff its citizens were made of and the reason why this nation has become such a great and wonderful country.

Through the success of *The Birth of a Nation* the two-dollar movie was born. But here let there be no misunderstanding: the two-dollar-a-seat innovation in the movies was H. E. Aitken's idea. He was opposed in it by both Mr. Griffith and Mr. Dixon, Mr. Dixon becoming so alarmed that he type-wrote a twelve-page argument against it. However, Mr. Aitken persisted and the result proved him right. The public will pay if they think your show is worth it.

Through the success of *The Birth of a Nation*, the sole habitat of the movies was no longer Eighth Avenue, Sixth Avenue, Avenue A and Fourteenth Street; the movies had reached Broadway to stay. D. W. Griffith had achieved that, and had he stopped right there he would have done his bit in the magical development of the motion picture. For though *Bagdad Carpets* fly, and *Ten Commandments* preach, and *Covered Wagons*[6] trek—miles and miles of movies unreel, and some of them awfully fine—they must all acknowledge that the narrow trail that led to their highway was blazed by Mr. Griffith.

---

[4] *The Escape* was DWG's second film for Reliance-Majestic. It received its première at the Cort Theatre, New York, June 1, 1914. Blanche Sweet, Mae Marsh, and Robert Harron starred.

[5] March 3, 1915. It was the first public showing of the film under this title. With the title *The Clansman*, it had already been presented on February 8, 1915, at Clune's Auditorium, Los Angeles, California.

[6] The allusions here are to celebrated films of the twenties: Douglas Fairbanks' *The Thief of Bagdad* (1923–24), DeMille's first version of *The Ten Commandments* (1923), and James Cruze's *The Covered Wagon* (1923). These films were current successes at the time Mrs. Griffith was writing the book from which the excerpt is taken.

Griffith and THE BIRTH OF A NATION
by A. NICHOLAS VARDAC

. . . Griffith, no longer with Biograph, was attracted by Thomas Dixon's successful stage melodrama, *The Clansman*, dealing with the South, the Civil War, and the Reconstruction period. Eager to challenge the success of European spectacle films, Griffith was excited by the spectacular productional opportunities of the play. Mutual refused to finance the production in the scale of Griffith's conception. A new corporation was formed under the name of Epoch Films, and *The Clansman* was filmed in twelve reels at the cost of $100,000. Released in 1915, it ran for forty-five consecutive weeks in New York alone, and within the next few years grossed $18,000,000. This production, rechristened *The Birth of a Nation*, was a phenomenal artistic as well as financial success. Its methods expressed an ultimate in motion-picture achievement, clarifying the antecedents of the film and forecasting its future.

The Birth of a Nation embodied three qualities which were responsible for its success and thus exerted a significant influence on the art of the film: (1) full utilization of the action-melodrama editorial technique, (2) great authenticity in setting and in acting, and (3) spectacle on a colossal scale. One quality supported the other, and in the mutual assistance the whole arose to a new level in cinematic expression.

In editorial technique Griffith did not alter his methods; he merely intensified them. Cutting in all directions, backward, forward, and across, transitions through clever camera devices, dynamic use of productional values and of the camera to build the scene and to control

Reprinted by permission of the publishers from A. Nicholas Vardac,
Stage to Screen (*Cambridge, Mass.: Harvard University Press*), *pp. 223–25. Copyright 1949 by the President and Fellows of Harvard College.*

the over-all development of dramatic intensity, all were brilliantly welded to surpass Griffith's previous efforts. His use of the single shot as an editorial unit was recognized for its effectiveness in development of climax by Henry MacMahon, early screen critic of the *New York Times*. "Every little series of pictures, continuing from four to fifteen seconds, symbolizes a sentiment, a passion or an emotion. Each successive series, similar yet different, carries the emotion to the next higher power, till at the last, when both of the parallel emotions have attained the swift shock of victory and defeat."[1] With such an intensively developed editorial technique, Griffith spared no effort to achieve realistic and spectacular melodrama.

The authenticity and scale of graphic values Griffith now knew to be the greatest appeal of motion-picture spectacle.

Sets were all constructed according to elaborate research which had been conducted for some time previous to starting work on the picture. The result of this research was the installing of the first research library in the picture business. All properties such as weapons, uniforms, furniture, costumes and also personal characteristics of leading characters like Sumner, Grant, Lee and Abraham Lincoln were carefully modelled on the best obtainable data in which every effort was made to have the picture authentic as an historical document.[2]

The care exercised in preparations for the production bore fruit. For instance, the assassination of Lincoln at Ford's Theatre,

with the play *Our American Cousin* going forward on the stage, is shown in careful accordance with the historical accounts of it. How Lincoln's guard left his post to get a view of the play; how Booth, waiting in the rear of another box, slipped through the door in the interval and fired at the president as he watched the play, all are seen. Booth's leap to the stage and his escape in the sudden excitement are faithfully portrayed.[3]

It was this sort of thing that audiences trained in the melodrama and the spectacle of the nineteenth century now looked for and ex-

---

[1] *New York Times*, June 6, 1916.
[2] From a lecture by Frank Woods entitled "Growth and Development," delivered February 27, 1929, at the University of Southern California; included in the unpublished "Introduction to Photoplay" (Los Angeles: Academy of Motion Picture Arts and Sciences: 1929), pp. 25–26.
[3] *New York Sun*, March 4, 1915.

pected in the film. And it was this sort of thing that the film could best do. In the war scenes of *The Birth of a Nation* this facility was spectacular. "Troops charging, artillery trains galloping, flags waving, shells bursting over barricades, the flow of battle over a field miles in length, are shown in full detail; and immediately after the excitement of the charge there is the sight of trenches full of torn and mangled bodies." [4] The illusion of authenticity in this daring motion picture, treating with realism the racial problems of the South from the clansman's bias, moved people "to cheers, hisses, laughter and tears, apparently unconscious and subdued, by tense interest in the play; they clapped when the masked riders took vengeance on Negroes, and they clapped when the hero refused to shake the hand of a mulatto who had risen by political intrigue to become lieutenant-governor." [5]

The authenticity given its production resulted in such a realistic illusion that controversies immediately sprang up. Harvard's President Eliot condemned its "tendency to perversion of white ideals." [6] Race riots occurred in Boston. The *New York Evening Post* labeled it "An appeal to race prejudice," and in the same breath explained this appeal as "a thrilling historic spectacle of battles and life of the days of the Civil War, and an explanation of Southern feeling in the reconstruction days in defense of the Ku Klux Klan which terrorized Negroes during that period." [7] But on the following day, the Reverend Thomas B. Gregory defended the film on the basis of its authenticity against all charges of exaggerated and malicious propaganda. "I know it is true," he said, "because I lived through the actual realities themselves. . . . I am prepared to say that not one of the more than five thousand pictures that go to make up the wonderful drama is in any essential way an exaggeration. They are one and all faithful to historic fact, so that looking upon them, *you may feel you are beholding that which actually happened.*" [8] The italics are my own to draw attention again to the fact that while Griffith exploited both melodrama and spectacle it was the authenticity of his production that enlarged its emotional power. By virtue of this quality, long-past truths, melodramatically treated, appeared as current actualities. If the popularity of the film had been secured in 1902 on the basis of simple melodrama, its establishment in 1915 as a full-fledged and autonomous art form came through the

[4] Ibid.
[5] Ibid.
[6] Terry Ramsaye, *A Million and One Nights* (New York: Simon and Schuster, 1926), p. 643.
[7] *New York Evening Post*, March 4, 1915.
[8] *New York American*, March 5, 1915.

D. W. Griffith at the pinnacle of his career.

Lillian Gish (left) as the heroine in Griffith's Biograph film, *The Musketeers of Pig Alley* (1912).

Blanche Sweet (right) as Judith and Lillian Gish (left) as The Little Mother in Israel in Griffith's first multireel epic picture, *Judith of Bethulia* (made in 1913, released the following year).

The famous "mooning sentry" scene in *The Birth of a Nation* (1915). William Freeman, as the sentry, gazes longingly at Lillian Gish, who plays Elsie Stoneman, the heroine.

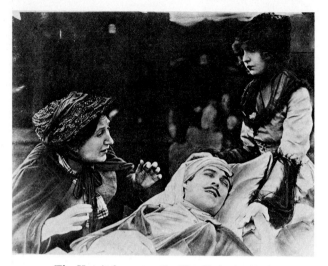

The Hospital sequence in *The Birth of a Nation* (1915). Mrs. Cameron (played by Josephine Crowell) visits a Federal hospital and finds that her wounded son, The Little Colonel (played by H. B. Walthall), has been sentenced to death. Lillian Gish, as the girl he loves, hovers in the background.

Walter Long as Gus, the renegade Negro, seized by the Klan for attempting to rape Flora Cameron, the heroine's "pet sister," and driving her to her death, in *The Birth of a Nation*.

The most spectacular of sets—constructed for the scenes
of Belshazzar's Feast in *Intolerance* (1916).

United Artists Corporation is signed into existence (1919). At the meeting are Griffith (left) holding a document, Mary Pickford (center), Charlie Chaplin (pen in hand), and Douglas Fairbanks (extreme right).

G. W. "Billy" Bitzer at the camera while Griffith (right) directs a scene in *Way Down East* (1920).

Griffith directs Lillian Gish in a scene in *Way Down East* (1920).

fusion of authentically spectacular production with this melodramatic structure. This fusion, when we consider, for instance, the poor reception given *The Clansman* at the Liberty Theatre, New York, in 1906, superseded similar activity in spectacle and melodrama on the stage. . . .

The Simplicity Of True
Greatness
by PAUL O'DELL

Violent controversy has surrounded Griffith's first major independent motion picture right from the evening of February 8, 1915 when it was premiered under the title of one of the books on which it was based, *The Clansman.* As *The Birth of a Nation,* it opened early in the following month in New York. This gigantic picture, conceived in terms hitherto undreamt-of in the sphere of the photoplay drama, was on such a scale and of such dramatic intensity that it demonstrated for the first time the terrific—and terrifying—potential of the cinema. Griffith had created a film which was to remain a constant work of reference for film students and film-makers throughout the world. Even after fifty-five years the film still retains a freshness and vitality, quite apart from the positively exhausting dramatic content. This does in some way explain how, within a period of twenty-five years following its initial release, the film had made its own production cost almost fifteen times over. Kevin Brownlow has made the observation that film students, "expecting an earth-shattering masterpiece, are shown a scarcely visible museum piece. They cannot know that it bears about as much relation to the original as a shrivelled husk bears to a once-fabulous butterfly." This taken into consideration, the film still has the unmistakeable stamp of genius of a director who understands his medium, and the fact that the manner of its presentation still manages to stir up the muddy controversy of racialism bears witness to the film's durability. It is certainly true that dupe after dupe have steadily decreased the original crispness of the image, and the subtle tones of "Billy" Bitzer's photography have turned gradually into the soot-and-whitewash blur that

From The Silent Picture (*London*), *no. 4* (*Autumn, 1969*), *pp. 18–20. Copyright 1969 by Mr. Paul O'Dell and* The Silent Picture. *Reprinted by permission of the author.*

many have come to accept, sadly, as the norm for all films made prior to, say, 1920.

To understand *The Birth of a Nation* as an historical motion picture, it is necessary to put it in the context of the kind of pictures which were being made at that time and immediately previous to its release. This is a subject which requires more space than is available here. To understand *The Birth of a Nation* as the first of Griffith's masterworks, however, it is necessary first to understand the nature of his work up until the date of its production. Griffith had felt no particular urge to make motion pictures at the start of his career; and *The Birth of a Nation* was by no means the product of a talent who could not help but make masterpieces every time he made a film. He had been involved in film production for some eight years previous, and had already directed something like 500 pictures, mostly one-reelers for American Biograph but including four more ambitious films made for Reliance-Majestic immediately preceding the production of *The Birth of a Nation*. Since his first film for Biograph, made way back in the summer of '08, he had utilized the great number of films in which he had been involved since then to develop ideas and techniques, dramatic situations and visual effects, which he was to expand and use with more subtlety—due to the dimensions of his major works after 1915—than he had been able to do within the rigid framework of the AB one-reelers. Each new experiment tends to stand out as if the whole film might have been built around it in the one-reelers; but by the time those experiments reemerge in the large-scale films they have become integral parts of the whole dramatic structure. They work more effectively for being able to contribute to the general narrative, instead of appearing as outstanding examples of cinematic technique; although the fact that this is precisely what they are is one of which we should not lose sight.

Cross-cutting, or switching from one narrative thread to another to achieve a heightened dramatic result, had been used by Griffith—if not entirely pioneered by him—as early as 1909 in a surprisingly complex picture called *The Drive for a Life*. But even there the simplest use of this technique could not help but take up a good third of the whole film's duration, leaving precious little time for any serious development of the central dramatic situation. By the time Griffith was using it in 1913, in *The Battle at Elderbush Gulch,* which was a two-reeler, he had become infinitely more sophisticated in his use of cross-cutting. Here he introduces more narrative threads than two, and the pace is more carefully controlled, giving the film a delicate balance as it switches from one set of characters in one situation to another set in a complementing scene. In *Intolerance* four years later he brought this treatment to its zenith, and in *The Birth of a Nation* the closing sequences obviously benefit enormously from Griffith's practical exploration of the technique in the earlier ABs.

It is very tempting to construct elaborate and penetrating theories arising from the construction, both dramatically and technically, of any motion picture. But Griffith's unfortunate (for us) habit of travelling across the American continent recutting his film after each performance, according to the reaction of that particular evening's audience, makes it very difficult—and dangerous—to analyze in depth a picture which today may bear very little resemblance to the director's original intention. Kevin Brownlow's contention that the film is a pale shadow of its former self can only seem the more painfully true in the light of this knowledge. One can only speculate.

In relation to the films for American Biograph that immediately precede Griffith's departure from the company, it is possible to see *The Birth of a Nation* as a natural progression. I must claim ignorance of the Reliance-Majestic pictures, but even on the basis of seeing the later ABs, it is easy to see Griffith's imagination spreading to larger, longer and more ambitious subjects, and his treatment of them taking on an aspect more suited for the kind of films he was obviously longing to make. One gets the impression of an imagination expanding in a restricted space—one reel was so insufficient as to be regarded by Griffith as almost worthy of contempt (he intimated as much later on) and even two reels can hardly have been expected to contain the breadth of his vision. Four reels—he only made one four-reel picture for American Biograph, *Judith of Bethulia*—is more suitable for his kind of film; and *Judith of Bethulia* betrays Griffith's passion for the epic. A Biblical theme, spectacular battle scenes involving many extras. But not treated as he had treated previous battle scenes, having to compromise to the maximum footage afforded by one reel. Here the battles are shown both in sweeping longshots and detailed close-up work. Revealing close shots and comprehensive panoramas give the overall scenes a greater reality than before, bringing out the drama more forcibly. The intimate scenes gain much from this new freedom; they are allowed to create their own pace, not cut down to a minimum but when the situation seems to demand it are allowed to run for what the Biograph front-office thought would *justify* a mass walk-out from the theatre, not only cause it. The production of this picture put the last nail in the coffin for Griffith at Biograph. He left, and the picture was not released. Not, that is, until the resounding success of *The Birth of a Nation,* some two years later, caused the Biograph management to think again. By that time, it was too late. Griffith's departure from them meant also the departure of many of their stock company—

the Gish sisters, Harron, Walthall, Mae Marsh among them—and the combination of both meant a slow but inevitable downhill path for the fortunes of the once illustrious and prosperous American Biograph Company.

Amid all this discussion on technique—valid and valuable though it undoubtedly is—one should not overlook the fact that Griffith was first and foremost a dramatist. He had ambitions as a playwright before he entered movies, and the sense of the theatrical is always present in his films. It is this feeling for the basic, dramatic construction of any given scene which is, in the last analysis, more important than the technique applied to it. There is a scene in *The Birth of a Nation,* often quoted but with some justification, where Ben Cameron, returning from a military hospital in Washington to his home in the South, is greeted by his younger sister and mother. It has been called a stroke of genius that throughout the entire scene we never see the mother; Ben stands on the threshold, and his mother's arm appears from behind the open door, motioning him in, enfolding him, welcoming him home after the war. But there is more to the scene than simply this. The scene consists basically of two shots, both allowed to run longer than one's patience would normally accept. The first shot alone runs almost a full minute in length, which is extremely long by the standards of the day. This shot begins with Ben's sister running out to meet him (played by Mae Marsh). They look at each other for a long time; Ben hasn't seen her since she was a young child—now she's a woman. She remarks on his dirty uniform, he on her pathetic attempts to "dress up" by marking lumps of wool with coal dust to make "Southern Ermine." She then notices a bullet hole in his hat. They both reflect on the past few years—and the horror of war, the disaster of its aftermath touches them both with frightening reality. Suddenly she breaks into tears and they embrace, he gently kissing her hair. Now the shot changes and the one described previously follows. A full twenty seconds long, with virtually no action within the frame. Griffith the dramatist replaces Griffith the technician, allows the drama of the scene to play out its full and natural length, create its own pace and pathos, and in so doing produces a scene of rare emotional qualities.

There are many other examples of this economy of technique: following the title *"The Last of Their Possessions to be Sold for the Failing Cause"* is a scene in which Miriam Cooper and Mae Marsh part with their best dresses but decide in the end that the fact that they now appear poor and ragged is of no consequence in view of the cause to which they are contributing. The scene in which the Cameron family receive the news of the death of their second son is another example. In one long shot, lasting a full minute, the full tragedy of the situation is imparted through the actors' and actresses' skill and Griffith's manipulation of them. It is worth noting, on the subject of Griffith's handling of his actors and actresses, what Miss Mae Marsh had to say: "Everything—scenery and players—is just so many instruments in his orchestra." This should not be taken as indicative of a fondness on Griffith's part for showing authority arbitrarily however. "Mr. Griffith," Miss Marsh continues, "is extremely human. There is no unnecessary flourish, or blowing of trumpets, about his manner of direction. That has the simplicity of true greatness. He never lords it over his players as I have seen some directors do. He is kindly, sympathetic and understanding." "We always had the wonderful feeling," she says, "that he was intensely loyal to all of us."

The long scene in which Ben refuses to shake hands with Lynch is also worth studying for Griffith's use of static camera and long action within a continuous shot. But perhaps the finest sequence, in which this approach is employed, is that in which Flora jumps from a cliff and is killed as she falls. In three shots Griffith establishes the strong feelings which lead eventually to the final "retaliation" of the Ku Klux Klan against Silas Lynch and his henchmen. A beautiful and tender sequence, showing Ben finding the broken body of his younger sister, carrying her home and the reaction of the family. *"And None Grieved More than These"* is a title followed by the Negro servants of the family. It is interesting how this scene, which to many represents one of the more distasteful "racialist" elements of the film, compares with the original passage in Dixon's book *The Clansman*. In the film, Flora (Mae Marsh) is chased by the Negro Gus (Walter Long), and in her girlish terror falls into a ravine. In the book however, Flora is raped by a Negro, and her mother sees no other honorable course than for the both of them to commit suicide. Therefore, they both throw themselves from the cliff-top voluntarily and purposely. It is a disgusting passage and is not even redeemed by any other part of the work, which is so blatantly racist as to leave a very unpleasant taste in one's mouth. The same cannot be said of *The Birth of a Nation* which by comparison (though odious) is all impartiality. Seymour Stern, noted Griffith historian, has stated that Griffith consulted over a dozen literary and historical sources of reference and based Part II more on these than on Dixon's novels. (I have not read *The Leopard's Spots*.)

The political implications of the film are not ones I care to discuss at length for I firmly believe that Griffith was certainly no racialist and made the film in the knowledge that he was presenting a true and accurate picture in dramatic terms. His reply to his adversaries—his next picture and I believe his greatest single achievement—was the cinema's first great plea for tolerance and understanding. In an introductory title to *The Birth of a Nation* Griffith puts his case:

We do not fear censorship, for we have no wish to offend with improprieties or obscenities, but we do demand, as a right, the liberty to show the dark side of the wrong, that we may illuminate the bright side of virtue. . . .

Fighting a Vicious Film: Protest Against THE BIRTH OF A NATION

In its advertisement we are told that *The Birth of a Nation* is founded on Thomas Dixon's novel *The Clansman*; that it is a war play "that worked the audience up into a frenzy"; that "it will make you hate."

In an interview with a Boston editor, Thomas Dixon said, "that one purpose of his play was to create a feeling of abhorrence in white people, especially white women, against colored men"; "that he wished to have all Negroes removed from the United States and that he hopes to help in the accomplishment of that purpose by *The Birth of a Nation.*

In furthering these purposes the producers of the film do not hesitate to resort to the meanest vilification of the Negro race, to pervert history and to use the most subtle form of untruth—a half truth.

Well knowing that such a play would meet strong opposition in Boston, large sums of money were spent in the employment of Pinkerton detectives and policemen to intimidate citizens, and the managers of the theatre refused to sell tickets to colored people. To soften opposition, the impression was given that the president of the United States had endorsed the play and that George Foster Peabody and other distinguished people favored it. One method of working up support was to pass cards among the auditors asking them to endorse the play. These cards were circulated, signed and collected at the end of the first act and before the second act in which appear the foul and loathsome misrepresentations of colored people and the glorification of the hideous and murderous band of the Ku Klux Klan.

The indignation against the play grew in intensity. The colored people of greater Boston rose in mass against it. It was opposed by many distinguished citizens including Governor Walsh, Lieutenant-

From Fighting a Vicious Film: Protest Against *The Birth of a Nation,* (*Boston, Mass.: Boston Branch of the National Association for the Advancement of Colored People, 1915*), *47-page pamphlet.*

Governor Cushing, Mr. Moorfield Storey, Hon. Albert E. Pillsbury, Hon. Samuel W. McCall, Rev. Samuel M. Crothers, D.D., Dr. Alexander Mann of Trinity Church, a majority of both branches of the legislature and many religious and civic organizations. A series of public meetings, remarkable for the spirit of unity and brotherhood and a very pronounced desire to save every group of our varied citizenship from insult and indignity, resulted in securing a new Censor Law for the City of Boston. . . .

Disregarding this law, plainly intended to stop the play, two of the censors refused to revoke its license. . . .

The failure of the censors to stop *The Birth of a Nation* would have been a very grievous disappointment if the agitation against it had not brought good of a very deep and satisfactory kind. To learn that on a question of decency and self-respect they could get together and in a dignified, law-abiding manner resent, as one man, the insult offered to their race by this play was a wonderfully heartening result to the twenty thousand colored people of greater Boston. . . . With a view to giving some idea of the scope of the agitation and the spirit in which it was conducted a few of the many letters, resolutions and speeches produced by the opposition to the play in April are put in permanent form with the further purpose of aiding other communities in opposing this and all such productions. . . .

Analysis by Francis Hackett

If history bore no relation to life, this motion picture drama could well be reviewed and applauded as a spectacle. As a spectacle it is stupendous. It lasts three hours, represents a staggering investment of time and money, reproduces entire battle scenes and complex historic events; amazes even when it wearies by its attempt to encompass the Civil War. But since history does bear on social behavior, *The Birth of a Nation* cannot be reviewed simply as a spectacle. It is more than a spectacle. It is an interpretation, the Rev. Thomas Dixon's interpretation, of the relations of the North and South and their bearing on the Negro. . . .

In *The Birth of a Nation* Mr. Dixon protests sanctimoniously that his drama "is not meant to reflect in any way on any race or people of today." And then he proceeds to give to the Negro a kind of malignity that is really a revelation of his own malignity.

Passing over the initial gibe at the Negro's smell, we early come to a negrophile senator whose mistress is a mulatto. As conceived by Mr. Dixon and as acted in the film, this mulatto is not only a minister to the senator's lust but a woman of inordinate passion, pride and savagery. Gloating as she does over the promise of "Negro equality," she is soon partnered by a male mulatto of similar brute characteristics. Having established this triple alliance between the "uncrowned king," his diabolic colored mistress and his diabolic colored ally, Mr. Dixon shows the revolting processes by which the white South is crushed "under the heel of the black South." "Sowing the wind," he calls it. On the one hand we have "the poor bruised heart" of the white South, on the other "the new citizens inflamed by the growing sense of power." We see Negroes shoving white men off the sidewalk, Negroes quitting work to dance, Negroes beating a crippled old white patriarch, Negroes slinging up "faithful colored servants" and flogging them till they drop, Negro courtesans guzzling champagne with the would-be head of the Black Empire, Negroes "drunk with wine and power," Negroes mocking their white master in chains, Negroes "crazy with joy" and terrorizing all the whites in South Carolina. We see the blacks flaunting placards demanding "equal marriage." We see the black leader demanding a "forced marriage" with an imprisoned and gagged white girl. And we see continually in the background the white Southerner in "agony of soul over the degradation and ruin of his people."

Encouraged by the black leader, we see Gus the renegade hover about another young white girl's home. To hoochy-coochy music we see the long pursuit of the innocent white girl by this lust-maddened Negro, and we see her fling herself to death from a precipice, carrying her honor through "the opal gates of death."

Having painted this insanely apprehensive picture of an unbridled, bestial, horrible race, relieved only by a few touches of low comedy, "the grim reaping begins." We see the operations of the Ku Klux Klan, "the organization that saved the South from the anarchy of black rule." We see Federals and Confederates uniting in a Holy War "in defence of their Aryan birthright," whatever that is. We see the Negroes driven back, beaten, killed. The drama winds up with a suggestion of "Lincoln's solution"—back to Liberia—and then, if you please, with a film representing Jesus Christ in "the halls of brotherly love."

My objection to this drama is based partly on the tendency of the pictures but mainly on the animus of the printed lines I have quoted. The effect of these lines, reinforced by adroit quotations from Woodrow Wilson and repeated assurances of impartiality and goodwill, is to arouse in the audience a strong sense of the evil possibilities of the Negro and the extreme propriety and godliness of the Ku Klux Klan. So strong is this impression that the audience invariably applauds the refusal of the white hero to shake hands with a Negro, and under the circumstances it cannot be blamed. Mr. Dixon has identified the Negro with cruelty, superstition, insolence and lust. . . .

Whatever happened during Reconstruction, this film is aggressively vicious and defamatory. It is spiritual assassination. It degrades the censors that passed it and the white race that endures it.

PURPOSE OF THE FILM

I, Rolfe Cobleigh, of Newton, in the County of Middlesex and Commonwealth of Massachusetts, being duly sworn depose and say, that:

I am associate editor of *The Congregationalist* and *Christian World,* published at 14 Beacon St., Boston, where our offices are located.

My attention was attracted to the moving picture play entitled, *The Birth of a Nation,* by editorials which appeared in the *New York World, the New York Evening Post,* the *New York Globe* and other newspapers condemning the production when it was first shown in New York. Several of my friends, who saw the show in New York, soon reported to me their disapproval on the grounds that it incited race prejudice against the Negro race, that it glorified lynching and falsified history. Influenced by this evidence I wrote a letter to Mr. D. W. Griffith, who was advertised as the producer of the film, and protested against the exhibition of such a series of moving pictures as these were represented to be. I received in reply a letter from Mr. Thomas Dixon, whose interest in *The Birth of a Nation* was indicated by the paper upon which he wrote, the letter-head being printed with the words: "Thomas Dixon's Theatrical Enterprises," under which was *The Birth of a Nation,* with D. W. Griffith, following the titles of five other plays written by Mr. Dixon. He said in the letter referring to "our picture": "The only objection to it so far is a Negro Society which advises its members to arm themselves to fight the whites." He also wrote that Rev. Charles H. Parkhurst, D.D., was "making a report on this work," and that if I would "await Dr. Parkhurst's report" he would send it to me. This letter was dated March 27.

Under date of April 3, I wrote in reply: "I shall await Dr. Parkhurst's report, which you say you will send me, with interest." I asked for the name of "a Negro society which advises its members to arm themselves to fight the whites."

Mr. Dixon wrote again under date of April 5, enclosing Dr. Parkhurst's report of which he said: "As this letter has been forwarded to Mayor Curley by Dr. Parkhurst I will appreciate it if you will publish it in *The Congregationalist,* with any comment you may make. Also Dr. Gregory's letter except one clause." Both the Parkhurst and Gregory letters were in approval of *The Birth of a Nation.* Mr. Dixon referred to his opponents as a "Negro Intermarriage Society," a term used in Mr. Gregory's letter to Mayor Curley and he gave the name of the organization as the National Association for the Advancement of Colored People, and suggested that it might produce a play to answer him, and that, "The silly legal opposition they are giving will make me a millionaire if they keep it up." I did not reply to this letter.

On the morning of April 9, 1915, Thomas Dixon called at my office and I had a long talk with him about *The Birth of a Nation*. He tried to convince me that it deserved my approval. He referred especially to the favorable reports of Dr. Parkhurst and Mr. Gregory. Mr. Dixon asked what I thought of Dr. Parkhurst's approval of the play. I replied that the evidence which had come to me was so strongly against the play that I was not influenced by Dr. Parkhurst, but that I would try to judge the play impartially when I saw it. He talked at length with reference to the artistic and dramatic merits of the play and of its value for the teaching of history, and ridiculed those who disapproved it. In reply to my questions with reference to the treatment of the Negro race in the play, he said that the subject was a debate, that he presented one side and that those who disagreed were at liberty to present the other side.

Mr. Dixon admitted that some of the scenes as originally presented in New York were too strongly suggestive of immorality and that he told Mr. Griffith they went too far.

I asked Mr. Dixon what his real purpose was in having *The Birth of a Nation* produced, what he hoped to accomplish by it. He began to read from the copy of Thomas B. Gregory's letter to Mayor Curley six things that Mr. Gregory said the play did in its effect on an audience. I interrupted to say, "Yes, but what is your chief purpose, what do you really want to accomplish through the influence of this play?" He replied in substance that he wanted to teach the people of the United States, especially the children, that the true history of the Reconstruction period was as it was represented in *The Birth of a Nation*. He said that in the play he presented the historical fact that Thaddeus Stevens became dictator of the United States government immediately after the death of President Lincoln, and that he appeared in the play under the name of Stoneman. Mr. Dixon said that one purpose in the play was to suggest Stevens' immorality in his relationship to his colored mistress for many years. He said the alleged sensual character of this woman, who in the play is called "Lydia Brown, Stoneman's mulatto housekeeper," was emphasized. Mr. Dixon described bad conditions in the South during the Reconstruction period, alleging that the Negroes gained control politically incited chiefly by Thaddeus Stevens, that the white Southerners were insulted, assaulted, robbed and disfranchised and that white girls and women were in constant danger of assault by colored men. He emphasized the alleged dominant passion of colored men to have sexual relations with white women and said that one purpose in his play was to create a feeling of abhorrence in white people, especially white women against colored men. Mr. Dixon said that his desire was to prevent the mixing of white and Negro blood by intermarriage. I asked him what he had to say about the mixing of the blood outside marriage and if it was not true that white men had forced their sexual relations upon colored girls and women all through the period of slavery, thus begetting children of mixed blood outside marriage, and if it was not true, as I am creditably informed, that such conditions prevail to a wide extent even among white men who occupy high social and political positions in the South today.

Mr. Dixon hesitated and finally answered that there was less of such conditions than there had been. Mr. Dixon said that the Ku Klux Klan was formed to protect the white women from Negro men, to restore order and to reclaim political control for the white people of the South. He said that the Ku Klux Klan was not only engaged in restoring law and order, but was of a religious nature, as represented in the play, having religious ceremonies and using the symbol of the cross. He said that the best white men of the South were in it, that Mr. Dixon's father was a Baptist minister in North Carolina and left his church to join the Ku Klux Klan, and that he remained with the organization until it was disbanded.

I asked Mr. Dixon what solution of the race problem he presented in *The Birth of a Nation* and he replied that his solution was Lincoln's plan. He said this was the colonization of the Negroes in Africa or South America, which he said President Lincoln favored during the last of the Civil War. Mr. Dixon said that he wished to have that plan carried out, that he wished to have all Negroes removed from the United States and that he hoped to help in the accomplishment of that purpose by *The Birth of a Nation*.

I suggested the difficulty of getting ten million people out of the country, and asked if he seriously advocated such a scheme. He replied with great earnestness that he did, that it was possible to create public sentiment such that a beginning could be made in the near future, that a large faction of the Negroes themselves would cooperate in the enterprise and that within a century we could get rid of all Negroes.

Mr. Dixon informed me that the first presentation of *The Birth of a Nation* in Boston would be given that evening for censorship before the mayor and other city officials and newspaper critics and gave me two tickets for that exhibition. He said that in anticipation of a hostile demonstration he and his associates would have thirteen Pinkertons scattered through the audience at the first performance and that as many or more Pinkertons would be employed in the Tremont Theatre at the exhibitions that would follow in Boston, with orders to rush anyone into the street instantly who started any disturbance. He said that he had feared there would be trouble in New York and that many Pinkertons were employed when the show was presented in New York, but that up to the time I saw Mr. Dixon there had been no disturbance in the Liberty Theatre, where the play was presented in New York. Mr. Dixon said that he owned a one-fourth interest in *The Birth of a Nation* Company.

I asked Mr. Dixon to what cities the show would be taken next and he replied that all plans had been held up until they knew the result of the protests in Boston. He said he regarded Boston as the critical point for their enterprise, that it was more likely to object to such a play than any other city and that he and his associates believe that if they could get by in Boston they would be able to go anywhere else in the country with the show without trouble.

As he went away he asked me to let him know what I thought of the play after I had seen it and expressed the hope that I would approve it.

I saw *The Birth of a Nation* that evening, April 9, and saw it again three weeks later, after omissions had been made to comply with the decision of Judge Dowd. I have expressed my disapproval of *The Birth of a Nation,* following each view of it on the grounds of falsifying history, in a riot of emotions glorifying crime, especially lynching, immorality, inviting prejudice against the Negro race, falsely representing the charactor of colored Americans and teaching the undemocratic, unchristian and unlawful doctrine that all colored people should be removed from the United States. I especially disapprove the play because Mr. Dixon frankly explained to me that his purpose in the play was to promote a propaganda with the desire to accomplish the results that I have stated.

ROLFE COBLEIGH

Personally appeared Rolfe Cobleigh and made oath to the truth of the foregoing affidavit by him subscribed before me in Boston, Massachusetts, this 26th day of May, A.D. 1915.

GEORGE R. BRACKETT,
Notary Public

Duty of the White South

. . . An author like Mr. Dixon and the producer, Mr. Griffith, ought to realize that if the Negro was as bad as they paint him in the film he was what the South made him; he was the shadow of her own substance; and pride of race, if there were any in the white South, ought to suppress this exposition of their own shame. . . .

WILLIAM STANLEY BRAITHWAITE

Portrays Negroes as Beasts

I, Oswald Garrison Villard, testify that I have witnessed the performance of *The Birth of a Nation* at the Liberty Theatre in New York, and that I unhesitatingly testify that I consider said production improper, immoral, and unjust to the colored people of the country. I further testify that if the matter of race were eliminated, the play would, in my judgment, as to the objectionable scenes at least, be unfit for public production, since there is a suggestiveness about it of the kind which physicians and alienists know too often incites to crime with certain types of minds. The attack upon the Negro in this play is entirely unnecessary; it is not directly related to the story, nor is it proportional to the space given to the big things with which the play deals. In my judgment it is a deliberate attempt to humiliate ten million American citizens, and to portray them as nothing but beasts. In my judgment the play should not be tolerated in any American city.

OSWALD GARRISON VILLARD

Gross Libel

This pictorial recrudescence of the rebellion is a gross libel upon the Union cause, upon its public leaders, Lincoln only excepted, upon every soldier, living or dead, who fought for it, and upon the whole people who supported it. Slavery and rebellion were right, the South was outraged by emancipation, the attempt to secure the Negro in his freedom was a crime for which wholesale murder was the proper remedy, the Negro was unfit for freedom and is unfit for civil rights, the Yankees were vandals, the rebels the true chivalry, and the Ku Klux Klan the heroes of the whole drama. This is the moral of the tale, conveyed with skillful innuendo and most consummate art. It gambles on the public ignorance of our own history, and as a vast majority of people are more impressed by what they see than by what they read or hear, it is liable to win by permanently lodging a radically false conception in the public mind.

A. E. PILLSBURY

Not Endorsed by the President

. . . Referring to your recent favor containing copies of statements in which it was claimed that President Wilson had given his endorsement and approval of the photoplay which was presented before the president some time ago called *The Birth of a Nation,* I beg to say that I called at the White House, and the president's secretary the Honorable J. P. Tumulty made a most emphatic denial of the above statement that the president had endorsed the play. I have today received from Mr. Tumulty the following letter:

THE WHITE HOUSE
Washington, April 28, 1915

My dear Mr. Thatcher:—

Replying to your letter and enclosures, I beg to say that it is true that *The Birth of a Nation* was produced before the president and his family at the White House, but the president was entirely unaware of the character of the play before it was presented and has at no time expressed his approbation of it. Its exhibition at the White House was a courtesy extended to an old acquaintance.

Sincerely yours,

(Signed) J. P. TUMULTY,
Secretary to the President

THREE MILES OF FILTH

It is three miles of filth. We believe this film teaches a propaganda for the purpose of so stirring up the people of the East and the West and the North that they would consent to allowing the Southern programme of disfranchisement, segregation and lynching of the Negro and finally to the repeal of the fourteenth and fifteenth Amendments to the Constitution.

HON. W. H. LEWIS

INTOLERANCE (1916)
by LEWIS JACOBS

Profound though its theme is, the commanding feature of *Intolerance* is its internal organization. Years ahead of its time (it was to become a major influence on the Soviet school of directors), *Intolerance* surpassed even *The Birth of a Nation*. The comparatively simple editing pattern of the latter film, based on one single event and story related in time and space, was in *Intolerance* expanded into a complex form with four movements, all progressing simultaneously. The film cuts freely from period to period as the theme of intolerance in each is developed. Episode is paralleled with episode. With bold, staccato cutting, Griffith interweaves the motifs of Christ struggling toward Calvary, the Babylonian mountain girl speeding to warn Belshazzar that his priests have betrayed him, the massacre on St. Bartholomew's Day by the French mercenaries, and Dear One rushing frantically to save her husband at the gallows.

These passages are vividly motivated by every means Griffith had at his disposal. A shot is cut before the completion of its action; the moving camera parallels and reinforces a movement; iris and masks are used to emphasize a significant detail or eloquently effect a transition; large detail close-ups and extreme long shots produce effects of intensity and vastness. All these camera devices are brought into play to create a rich and varied film which flows in unbroken and mounting suspense until the end. Here, as in *The Birth of a Nation,* an underlying movement creates a rhythmic beat, which increases in frequency as the four climaxes approach. There is not a moment, not a shot, that is not controlled, timed, and selected for what it means and adds to the whole.

In the climactic sequences, particularly, is Griffith's artistry supreme. Here all the opulent details of the lavish scenes are subjected to an un-

From Lewis Jacobs, The Rise of the American Film (*New York,* 1939; reprinted 1968), pp. 191–201 of the 1968 edition. Copyright 1968 by Lewis Jacobs. Reprinted by permission of Lewis Jacobs and Teachers College Press, Columbia University, New York.

ceasing movement, action follows action, and none is ever allowed to terminate as the rhythm sweeps along. Christ is seen toiling up Mount Calvary; the Babylonian mountain girl is racing to warn her king of the onrushing enemy; the Huguenot is fighting his way through the streets to rescue his sweetheart from the mercenaries; the wife is speeding in an automobile to the prison, with a pardon for her husband who is about to be hung.

Images whirl across the screen, startling the spectator with their pace and holding him spellbound by their profusion, rhythm, suspense. They are a visual symphony, swelling steadily until the final moment when all the movements are brought together in a grand finale. As Iris Barry wrote[1] of these passages, "History itself seems to pour like a cataract across the screen."

Individual episodes within each movement also have striking beauty of structure. At one point in the modern story for example, the reformers, whom Griffith satirically called Vestal Virgins of Reform, are shown going to workers' homes, led by a rich industrialist's wife who gives the workers charity and moral guidance, keeping them from drinking, gambling, and prostitution. Following this are scenes showing factory workers being shot down by militia called out by the industrialist.

This is one of the many striking episodes. . . . It is a vivid instance of Griffith's cutting. By an overlapping of movement from one shot onto the next, a double edge is given to the images and strong tension is created. Each shot, moreover, is cut to the minimum; it gives only the essential point. Facts build upon one another in the audience's mind until, in the very last shot, all the facts are resolved and summarized through the introduction of another type of shot, longer than any of its predecessors and significantly different in character. Not only the cutting and treatment of the sequences, but the deliberate documentary quality of the shots themselves, are remarkable. In this episode the origins of the remarkable Soviet technique are clearly evident.

As in its cutting, so in its details *Intolerance* had impressive originality. Huge close-ups of faces, hands, objects, are used imaginatively and eloquently to comment upon, interpret, and deepen the import of the scene, so that dependence upon pantomime is minimized. A celebrated instance is the huge close-up of the clasped hands of Mae Marsh, suggesting her anguish during the trial of her husband. Camera angles are used to intensify the psychological impact: the extreme long shot of the industrialist alone in his office (lord of his domain) characterized him better than any action, incident, or subtitle. The handling of crowds as organized units in movement, as in the firing of the militia

[1] Museum of Modern Art Film Library Program Notes (III).

or in the notable Babylonian sequences, heightened the dramatic intensity of such scenes. The deliberate use of artificial sky above the onrushing Persian chariots gave the panorama great depth and massiveness, heightening the sense of impending doom as no natural sky could have done, and incidentally introducing to film technique the "process shot."

The singling out of significant action on one part of the screen by lights, irises, or masks—examples of which appeared in almost every sequence—indicated Griffith's sensitive regard for the apt image. With admirable ease, he cuts daringly into the square shape of the screen and blocks out whole sections, sometimes leaving them blocked out for the duration of the scene, sometimes opening the frame to its size. But whether he uses it closed in or opened out, he rarely uses the same shape twice in succession, but contrasts them so that the eye of the spectator is kept moving. For example, if the screen opens in a semicircle from the lower right-hand corner to the upper left, as in the opening mass scene of Babylon, the next time, the screen opens in a semicircle from the upper left-hand corner, then opens out and down diagonally to the lower right.

This dramatic "framing" of the image throughout the film is done with a variety and skill that has rarely been equaled. The screen is sliced down the center revealing only the middle (the great wall of Babylon), then opens out. The screen is cut across diagonally, sometimes from upper left to lower right, sometimes from upper right to lower left. Details are thus brought to our attention and yet kept part of the larger scene itself in a more precise way than the use of close-up insertions could afford. This movement and variety of screen shapes keep the image ever-fresh and vital and heighten the momentum of the whole.

If the "framing" of the screen is remarkable, no less so is the fluid and active participation of the camera. Its physical capacities for movement and dramatic angle—generally conceded to be the original contributions of the postwar German craftsmen—must have strained to the taxing point whatever was known then of camera grace and flexibility. Yet there is never a sense of striving for sheer mechanical wonder, but always a subordination of such capabilities to the subject and the point to be made. The unceasing use of the camera to drain everything that is significant out of the scene, accounts in no small measure for the overwhelming sense of lavishness and opulence that is so impressive to all. For example, we are shown the court of France, 1572, first from an extreme long shot. The camera is stationary for a few moments as we take in the elaborate scene; then the camera begins slowly to "truck" into the court, moving in on King Charles receiving on his throne; then the camera "pans" to the right around the crowded room to pause on the Prince-Heir, who, incidentally, is portrayed as a decadent fop with a realism worthy of von Stroheim. Later in the film, in the marriage market of ancient Jerusalem, the camera "pans" to the right, showing the painted women framed in a diagonal strip across the screen from lower left to upper right. Again, in the Temple of Sacred Fire in Babylon, the camera plays caressingly over the white nudeness of erotic and sensual women clothed in flimsy chiffons, beflowered and bejeweled, by "panning" from right to left, then from left to right; then the screen frame closes in, then moves out, and in again with marvelous facility.

More spectacular than any of these devices, however, was the remarkable "trucking" camera shot which traveled, without a pause or a cut, hundreds of feet from an extreme distant view of the entire grandeur of ancient Babylon to a huge close-up of the scene itself. This shot, embracing immense sets, thousands of people and animals, was unprecedented and is still an amazing piece of camera bravura.

The film also utilized dramatically tinted film stock. Then a comparatively common device, it was seldom used on as large a scale or with as great variety. Night exteriors are tinted blue; sunny exteriors or lighted rooms are in various tones of yellow; blackness drapes the figures in the Temple of Sacred Fire; the Babylon battle at night is highlighted by red flares. Throughout the tints attempt to approximate reality; they show Griffith's awareness of the emotional values to be gained from the use of color.

With all its profound excellence, *Intolerance* nevertheless had many unfortunate weaknesses that marred its complete realization. The most obvious were Griffith's inherent sentimentality and his tendency to overdramatize. These weaknesses had appeared in *The Birth of a Nation* but, in view of that picture's subject and story, were less glaring. In *Intolerance* the maudlin names "little Dear One," "Brown Eyes," "Princess Beloved," all hangovers from the movies' past, are laughable. The extravagant posturing and the black-and-white characterizations are also hangovers from the prewar period. The massacre of the Huguenots and the Babylonian episode are full of bloodshed and violence, which reaches a ludicrous high when the soldier of Belshazzar cuts off the head of his enemy so that the audience can see it topple off (a scene that had appeared in *Judith of Bethulia* and the older *Mary, Queen of Scots,* and was apparently acceptable in its day). Griffith's overindulgence in pious, highly moral, and frequently saccharine explanatory titles is another defect.

The greatest fault of *Intolerance* was what Julian Johnson, reviewing the film for *Photoplay*,[2] was the first to comment upon: "The fatal er-

_____
[2] December, 1916.

ror of *Intolerance* was that in the great Babylonian scenes you didn't care which side won. It was just a great show." The overemphasis upon the spectacle outweighed the message. The formal concept ran away with the thematic; the execution was brilliant, but the point was forgotten. This discrepancy between the admirable structure and the uncertainty of the message is the reason why many people regard *The Birth of a Nation* as the greater of the two films. In that film one is forced, by the way the case is presented, to side with the South; in *Intolerance* the spectator is emotionally aroused but not as a partisan.

First shown publicly September 5, 1916, the film evoked mixed criticism. Many of the critics of the day were bewildered by the cutting style, could not follow the story from period to period, and were confused by the "interminable battle scenes" and the recurring "mother rocking her baby." They found the idea obtuse and the effects exhausting. Like other publications *Variety*,[3] giving it far less attention than that accorded *The Birth of a Nation,* called it "a departure from all previous forms of legitimate or film construction . . . so diffuse in the sequence of its incidents that the development is at times difficult to follow." Heywood Broun[4] declared that the bathing beauty spectacle *Daughter of the Gods* [1916], starring Annette Kellerman, "has the enormous advantage over *Intolerance* that it tells a story." Years later Pudovkin, in his book *Film Technique*,[5] praised Griffith's structural innovations in *Intolerance* but thought the film "so ponderous that the tiredness it created largely effaced its effect."

At the time of the picture's release something like a war spirit was growing in the nation, and people could not reconcile the pacific intentions of *Intolerance*—intentions which they understood mainly through its titles—with the current militarism. As the country moved closer to active participation in the war, opposition to the film grew more vigorous. Censured and then barred in many cities, the picture suffered a sad and ignoble fate. Although it stands as a milestone in the progress of the American film, for Griffith it proved to be a financial disaster of crippling proportions. Through its failure he lost his independence and, no doubt, much of his great zeal.

Modern criticism of *Intolerance* has been increasingly favorable. The film has been called "a timeless masterpiece" [6] (Richard Watts, Jr.): "the end and justification of that whole school of American cinematography" [7] (Iris Barry): "an opulence of production that has never been

[3] September 8, 1916.

[4] *The New York Tribune,* October 20, 1916.

[5] P. 8.

[6] Quoted in Program given at a Revival Showing, November, 1933, at 55th St. Playhouse.

[7] Museum of Modern Art Film Library Program Notes (III).

equaled" [8] (Frank S. Nugent). It has thus reclaimed its rightful position as a peak in American movie making, the consummation of everything that preceded it and the beginning of profound new developments in the motion picture art. Its influence has traveled around the world, touching directors in Germany, France, and Soviet Russia in particular. A testament to Griffith's maturity, it marked the end of his second and most brilliant period and the turning point in his career. Although continuing actively in movie making in the next years, and maintaining his high reputation, he was never again to equal *Intolerance,* or its predecessor, *The Birth of a Nation.*

[8] *New York Times,* March 8, 1936.

The Films of David Wark Griffith: The Development of Themes and Techniques in Forty-two of His Films
by RICHARD J. MEYER

Every creative artist in the history of mankind has been influenced by his environment. Whether his work demonstrates rebellion, reflection, or anti-art, it nevertheless is a product of that particular age which gave birth to its creator. Art is the sum total of all human experience and as such does not discover new thematic material down through the ages; yet in each century there are a few individuals who are given the rare opportunity to express themselves in a new medium. These geniuses have at their disposal a free art form; they are tied to the boundless stream of man's total consciousness in the development of art, but they are also linked to their contemporary surroundings, from which they never break away. Such a man was D. W. Griffith.

There is no disagreement among film historians and critics anywhere in the world that David Wark Griffith was the first giant of the new film art and that he paved the way for contemporary cinema. But some argument concentrates on whether he actually invented certain innovations or whether he was merely the first director to use them in a meaningful filmic manner. Such conjecture aside, what is paramount is that Griffith was the first man to create undeniable film masterpieces.

This study traces the development of Griffith's narrative themes and film techniques, using as primary source material forty-two of his films

Originally published in Film Comment, *IV, no. 2–3 (Fall/Winter, 1967). Reprinted (with changes and additions by Dr. Meyer) by permission of Richard J. Meyer and* Film Comment. *Dr. Meyer is Director of the School Television Service, WNDT, New York City.*

screened at the Museum of Modern Art in the spring and summer of 1965. Biographical material will be used only if pertinent, because of disagreements among biographers. Similarly, criticism by dozens of writers will be kept relevant.

Griffith initially attempted, unsuccessfully, to sell film stories. He entered the film business as an actor for Edwin S. Porter at the Edison studio in 1907. *Rescued from an Eagle's Nest* tells the story of a woodsman (Griffith) who rescues a baby from the nest after an eagle has captured it. At that time, film technique and acting had not changed much since Porter's *The Great Train Robbery* of 1903. The contrast between a painted backdrop and the real outdoor scenery in *Rescued from an Eagle's Nest* is still great, and the major improvement by Porter in *Rescued* is the use of overlapping action when Griffith goes down the cliff, with a cut to a reverse angle shot.

In 1908, Griffith succeeded in selling stories to the Biograph Company as well as acting in some. Actors were paid five dollars a day, but writers received fifteen dollars for a "scenario." He was given an opportunity to direct. *The Adventures of Dollie,* released July 14, 1908, was an immediate success and revitalized the insecure Biograph. Most of the films released by the company from then until December 1909 were made by Griffith and all of the major ones thereafter until 1913.[1] His output between 1908 and 1915 was about 440 films.[2] He averaged one film per week, working fourteen hours a day.

Readers will recall in *The Great Train Robbery* how Porter created parallel action by cross-cutting the bandits with shots of the gathering of the posse. Griffith commenced to improve Porter's technique of parallel action by tightening up his editing of these early Biographs. Almost immediately, he discovered other methods. His cameraman, Billy Bitzer, collaborated in these many innovations, but it was Griffith who served as the spark in this creative relationship.

By the time *A Drunkard's Reformation* was released (April 1, 1909), Griffith had brought financial success to Biograph as well as to himself. Linda Arvidson, secretly Mrs. Griffith, played the drunkard's wife in this one-reeler. The film uses the play within a play device. A heavy-drinking father with his child views a stage presentation about the evils of alcohol and resolves to reform. Besides the much-improved interior scenery, the firelight effect during the last shot was an innovation.

The Lonely Villa with Mary Pickford (June 10, 1909) was shot out of the studio, in New Jersey. The film gave a clear indication that this

[1] Iris Barry, *D. W. Griffith: American Film Master* (New York: The Museum of Modern Art, 1965), p. 11.

[2] Seymour Stern, "Griffith: Pioneer of the Film Art," *Introduction to the Art of the Movies,* edited by Lewis Jacobs (New York: The Noonday Press, 1960), p. 158.

director would be developing not only realistic settings and new styles in screen acting, but suspenseful climaxes that eventually would be labeled "the Griffith ending." Cross-cutting from the wife and daughters trapped by the villain to the father who comes to the rescue with the police was the finest example of editing to that time. The "last minute rescue" was to remain with Griffith throughout his career.

A social commentary, *A Corner in Wheat* (December 13, 1909), begins with farmers under great hardship planting wheat. A tycoon corners the market, causing privation to the populace, but he dies when he slips into one of his own grain elevators and is buried by the grain. The early films delighted in such irony. For the first time, there is a fade to black at the end of the film. Griffith and Bitzer closed the iris diaphragm of the camera for a fade-out originally to solve the problem of the screen kiss, according to Homer Croy.[3] However, Seymour Stern, self-styled Griffith "Boswell," disputes Croy's account vigorously.[4]

A Corner in Wheat has an effect of special interest. From a scene of business crooks at a gala party celebrating their financial coup, Griffith cuts to a "freeze" frame effect (using actors in a tableau) of poor people waiting in a breadline.

The players hold still for over 12 seconds to create the effect. The technique was devised by Griffith to point out the social implications by comparing wealthy revelers with the poor who are "frozen" as they wait in line for bread which cannot be purchased because of the doubling in price. From this "freeze" frame effect, Griffith cuts back again to the scene at the festivities.

The weakest Griffith film screened was *The Last Deal* (January 27, 1910). Except that the camera moves closer for a card game, the film shows lackluster technique. A man gambles away his money and his wife's jewels and embezzles from the bank. The wife's brother saves the loser by winning at cards and giving the money to his brother-in-law just in time to prevent his suicide. At the close, the errant husband tears up the deck of cards. The stall for time between the card game and the contemplated suicide is particularly dull.

Another social commentary with a violent death at the end, similar to *A Corner in Wheat,* was released on August 15, 1910. In *The Usurer* a man forecloses the mortgages of sick girls and old mothers, then revels with his ill-gotten wealth. Later he is locked in a vault while counting his coupons and dies of suffocation. The evicted families get back their furniture and their apartments. Cross-cutting is used extensively.

On March 23, 1911, the most advanced one-reeler of its time was re-

---

[3] Homer Croy, *Star Maker* (New York. Duell, Sloan and Pearce, 1959), p. 39.
[4] Seymour Stern, "Biographical Hogwash," *Films in Review,* May, 1959, pp. 284–96 and June–July, 1959, pp. 336–43.

leased by Biograph. *The Lonedale Operator*, with Blanche Sweet, was shot in California on location. The camera was mounted on the loco-motive and on many other placements that change frequently. The medium shot replaces the long shot while the tight close-up of the wrench, with which the telegraph girl holds evildoers at bay, achieves an unparalleled excitement. Griffith improved his cross-cutting by in-ter-cutting among three separate scenes. He also had actors walk to-ward the camera to give a feeling of screen depth. Each shot is short. The story concerns the last-minute rescue of a girl by her railwayman friend as she prevents thugs from stealing money.

Enoch Arden was an attempt by Griffith to make a two-reeler. Bio-graph did not permit its release as such and separated it into Part I (June 12, 1911) and Part II (June 15, 1911). It was thought that audi-ences would accept only twelve-minute film plots. Based on a poem, *Enoch Arden* did not adapt well. It tells the story of two men who vie for a girl. She marries Arden, who later departs on a voyage, leaving behind her and their children. He is shipwrecked and presumed lost, and after twenty years the widow marries the old rival. But Arden is rescued and comes home to discover secretly what has transpired. He dies without interfering with the new happy family. Abrupt cuts from medium shot to close-up are awkward, but the use of children at vari-ous stages of their growth to denote passage of time is quite effective.

A long shot with action in both the background and foreground is a feature of *Man's Genesis* (July 11, 1911). Realistic interiors are a vast improvement over the interior painted scenery of a few years earlier, and composition is better. *Man's Genesis* begins with a preacher telling two children a story about cavemen days. The scene fades to black, then fades in a scene where a strong caveman takes away the girl of a weaker caveman. He regains the girl by making a stone weapon. Befitting a film made on the eve of World War I, Griffith's concluding moral states that as man develops new and better weapons, he will have to develop more wisdom. The picture returns to the preacher and the children. Flash-back is accomplished by the fade to black and the fade-in.

Violence and action continued to dominate the Griffith one-reelers. In *The Miser's Heart* (November 20, 1911), a poor girl befriends a miser. Crooks threaten to kill her if he does not give them the combina-tion to his safe. The miser finally tells, but the rascals are caught after a hobo summons the police. Two typical Griffith elements emerge from this film: the poor hero or heroine; and the use of children as sentimental devices. The camera moves still closer to the action in *The Miser's Heart*.

A jump cut to indicate the passage of time—while a killer changes from a disguise to his own clothes—is a highlight of *A Terrible Dis-*

covery (December 21, 1911). The killer, dressed as a woman, sneaks into the house in order to kill the boy's father (who has an artificial arm). The father lowers the boy out of a window to summon help as the killer breaks into the room. In a typical Griffith ending, the police race to rescue the dad, who is saved just as he is about to be shot. One criticism of Griffith has been that his humor was crude. In *The Goddess of Sagebrush Gulch* and other films, he used humor to relieve the tension of his melodramatic Victorian plots and to add an artistic touch. Broad laughter, within limits, is in the American tradition of humor and is not "crude" within that context. *The Goddess of Sagebrush Gulch* (March 25, 1912) depicts a Western girl who loses her boyfriend, the sheriff, to a female visitor from the East. The latter asks the sheriff for his money, then villains take the cash, tie her up, and set fire to the house. She is rescued after the rejected heroine runs for the sheriff. The crooks are killed in a gun battle, and the Western girl walks off with a successful prospector. Realistic mountain scenery, beautifully photographed, makes the film technically good, but the story is below Griffith's standards.

Apparently Griffith realized that *The Lonedale Operator* was one of his most successful films, because he remade it a year later as *The Girl and Her Trust* and improved on the original. It was released March 28, 1912. The tracking shot was achieved by placing the camera on a train while photographing another train. Griffith also had the camera pan during the moving shot. Through cross-cutting, he heightened suspense as the boyfriend rescues the telegraph girl.

The best Griffith one-reeler is *The Musketeers of Pig Alley*. The story and action of this film, released October 31, 1912, are exciting even by today's standards. Griffith incorporated not only violence and death, but also the social problems of his time. Shot in the back alleys of New York, the film had the look of the Ash Can School of art. If one looks for the predecessor of *Open City* and Italian neorealism, he may find it in *The Musketeers of Pig Alley*. The story, set in the slums, opens with a poor musician leaving his wife and mother to find work. He returns with money, but it is stolen by thieves. In a gang fight, he gets back his money. When the police ask him to identify the chief hoodlum, he protects him because the hood had protected his wife in an earlier bar incident. The final scene shows a cop winking at the hood and a hand reaching into the frame with money for him. The closing title announces—"Links in the system."

Six weeks later, another Griffith early masterpiece was released on December 15, 1912. *The New York Hat* possessed a good story as well as fine acting for the period. Lionel Barrymore and Mary Pickford starred, and Mae Marsh, Mabel Normand, and Lillian and Dorothy

Gish rounded out the cast. The minister (Barrymore) buys a girl an expensive hat with money left secretly to her by her deceased mother. Small-town gossips wag tongues about the minister until the mother's letter, which explains the situation, is revealed.

The God Within, released eleven days later, uses an interesting device for dialogue scenes—trees and bushes serve as foreground during these medium shots. The plot is typically Victorian. A bad girl loses her baby at birth while a saintly girl dies giving birth. The doctor arranges for the live baby to live with the surviving mother. She is forced to choose between her old lover and the good widower. She chooses the latter "for the child's sake."

Using California scenery, *Olaf—An Atom* (May 19, 1913) starred Harry Carey. This one-reeler uses a moving camera and a great variety of camera placements, including one on top of a mountain looking down into a valley and another from inside a building looking through a doorway to action outside. A drifter helps a family in need and then silently goes on his way.

The end of one era and the beginning of another was signified by *Judith of Bethulia,* filmed in 1913 and released by Biograph March 8, 1914 as its last Griffith film. *Judith of Bethulia* was the first American four-reeler. Its style incorporated all of Griffith's previous techniques, refined them, and created new ones. The iris-out and the iris-in were used. Many shots had background movement with a still foreground. Excellent spatial depth was achieved by long shots with action both near and far. A gobo is created when branches part to expose a view of the Assyrian Army. Flashbacks are achieved by quick cuts. An "S" curve is used when the Israelites chase the Assyrians and fill the screen with hordes of soldiers stretching from one side of the frame to the other. Spectacular crowd and battle scenes are used for the first time in Griffith. He also masked off portions of the frame to achieve pictorial and psychological effects, in one case to block out a view that Holofernes does not want to see.

The story from the Old Testament relates how Judith saves Bethulia from the Assyrians by taking the head of their general. The tale is intercut with a subplot about Naomi and Nathan. She is captured by the Assyrians and is rescued by him after Judith's heroic deed.

Biograph and Griffith parted company in 1913 because he wanted to make longer, more spectacular films. He joined Reliance-Majestic, which distributed through the Mutual Film Corporation. Griffith took with him from Biograph his stock company of actors and cameraman Billy Bitzer. The days of the one-reeler were over.

At Biograph, it had been Griffith's practice to take advantage of natural surroundings and weather. He was to exploit these elements in many of his later films. Linda Arvidson, his first wife, remembered: "A beautiful sleet had covered the trees in Central Park, and we hurried out to photograph it, making up the scenario on the way." [5]

An era had passed. The skills that Griffith had acquired from the one-reelers would now provide a foundation for longer films, films that would demonstrate to the world that this new medium could be much more than mere entertainment.

Griffith produced, directed, and wrote four films for Mutual. *Home, Sweet Home* and *The Avenging Conscience* foreshadow both in technique and acting *The Birth of a Nation* and *Intolerance*. *Home, Sweet Home,* six reels, opened in New York May 17, 1914. It is made up of four separate stories linked in an epilogue. A common theme underlying the song, "Home, Sweet Home" binds the plots together. Part I tells about the writing of the ballad and of composer John Howard Payne's downfall. Part II takes place in the West with an Easterner bonded to a girl by the song. Part III shows hate between brothers who finally kill each other. The mother lives in order to bring up her remaining dull son. Part IV tells about a wife who remains faithful to her husband although tempted to have an affair with another man. Just as she is about to yield, she hears strains of "Home, Sweet Home" and is saved. In the epilogue Payne is in hell trying to get to his sweetheart in heaven who has died waiting for him. She flies around in heaven and finally—because of the contribution of Payne's song to the world—he is united with her.

This last allegorical section clearly foreshadows the one in *Intolerance,* while the sets, costumes, and cast are almost identical to those in *The Birth of a Nation.* Besides incorporating key lighting and many iris effects, Griffith introduced the tilt or pan down of the camera to start a scene and the tilt or pan up to end a scene. He again used the growth of children to denote the passage of time and the double exposure for a dramatic effect in heaven.

As Ingmar Bergman does today, Griffith had his own repertory company. Through various roles, large and small, Blanche Sweet, Lillian Gish, Mae Marsh, Henry Walthall, Robert Harron, Spottiswoode Aitken, Donald Crisp, and many others acquired depth and range. Similarly, as many of the Swedish director's films reflect the current *Zeitgeist,* so Griffith mirrored the Victorian concepts still prevalent as World War I began.

The Avenging Conscience, which opened in New York August 2, 1914, a month after shooting for *The Birth of a Nation* had begun, polished further Griffith's many techniques. He shifted the iris from character to character. The long shot is used for a picture-postcard ef-

[5] Linda Arvidson Griffith, "Early Struggles of Motion Picture Stars," *Film Flashes* (New York: Leslie-Judge Company, 1916), p. 5.

fect. Close-ups are used as sound effects and to heighten tension—e.g., a shoe kicking a door, and cuts from a pencil tapping to a clock pendulum to nervous hands. The double exposure is used effectively for the ghost scenes, the moon and cloud shots, and the religious sequences with Christ, Moses, and ghouls. The last action may have been achieved by masking portions of the lens rather than by double exposure. A precursor of the impressionistic montage occurs at the end of the film. From a shot of the lovers, Griffith cuts away to Pan and a nineteenth-century dance of children and animals.

The plot of *The Avenging Conscience* is weak. An uncle brings up his nephew to follow in his footsteps as a scholar. The boy wants to marry, but the uncle disapproves. The lad bids his sweetheart goodbye and then kills the uncle. He is discovered by a detective in a direct steal from Poe's "The Tell-Tale Heart." The boy hangs himself and his girl throws herself off a cliff. Suddenly a *deus ex machina* occurs—it was only a dream. The nephew wakes up and sees the uncle alive. The lovers are reunited and the old man permits marriage. "They all live happily ever after."

Griffith's next film was to have a most profound effect upon the future of motion pictures. Siegfried Kracauer wrote that the battle scenes in *The Birth of a Nation* have never been surpassed despite newer technical innovations.[6] Even Sergei Eisenstein, while calling the film "a celluloid monument to the Ku Klux Klan," recognized its director as the greatest master of parallel montage.[7] Terry Ramsaye does not blame the film for the subsequent rise of the Klan, but he credits Thomas Dixon's novel, *The Clansman*, for the success of both.[8] Whether, as some claim, Griffith contributed to the resurgence of the Klan or whether his film merely mirrored U. S. social attitudes, all critics agree that *The Birth of a Nation* raised the screen to the level of an art form.[9]

The major contribution of this film was not its financial success ($50-million overall gross)[10] but its demonstration to the world that film was the greatest medium for propaganda yet devised. Emotions evoked by audiences brought riots, praise, prejudice, and criticism. The original version opened as *The Clansman* in Los Angeles Febru-

[6] Siegfried Kracauer, *Theory of Film* (New York: Oxford University Press, 1965), p. viii.

[7] Sergei Eisenstein, "Dickens, Griffith, and the Film Today," *Film Form*, edited and translated by Jay Leyda (New York: Meridian Books, 1958), p. 234.

[8] Terry Ramsaye, *A Million and One Nights* (New York: Simon and Schuster, 1964), pp. 635–44.

[9] Bosley Crowther, "D. W. Griffith: The Most," *The New York Times*, April 25, 1965.

[10] Seymour Stern, "Griffith—*The Birth of a Nation*," Part 1, *Film Culture* (Spring–Summer, 1965), p. 72.

ary 8, 1915. It appeared in New York March 3, 1915 as *The Birth of a Nation*. Five weeks later 170 shots were removed because of pressure from Black groups and Major John Mitchel. According to Stern and Croy, those portions of the film deleted were the most violently anti-Negro.[11] The story lends itself to propaganda because it deals with history. A vast tale of the Civil War and Reconstruction, *The Birth of a Nation* uses the device of tracing one Southern and one Northern family throughout the period. The families are intertwined as was the nation in the 1860s. The heroic treatment given the rise of the Klan graphically illustrated that the motion picture was a dynamic force in the dissemination of pseudo-fact. In the fifty years since its release this film has been shown as true history to millions of schoolchildren. The writer recalls its use as a good example of the Reconstruction by a history professor in a large Midwestern university a few years ago.

The film technique of *The Birth of a Nation* was, for the most part, not new. Griffith had been developing his cinematic style for eight years. What was fantastic, however, was the total integration of all his major innovations. The use of the iris to highlight emotion was magnificent, such as in love scenes and in the pan from the iris shot of a mother with her children to the slow opening up on Sherman's troops. Split screens and masking the camera to create spatial and depth effects created a new language of film. Bitzer's camera was constantly moving —on a dolly as the Confederates danced at the farewell ball; elevated as troops marched below, under the hooves of Klan horses as they headed to the rescue; and high above the battlefields as soldiers fought. Composition and contrasts were as seen by Matthew Brady photographs. Silhouette shots of the Klan and the many "historical facsimiles" of real events captured the spirit of mid-nineteenth-century America. Griffith's use of double exposure to show the seating of the Black legislators was copied many times by early Soviet film-makers—indeed, so was his sophisticated parallel editing. The freeze frame effect that Griffith had developed in *A Corner in Wheat* was used to show dead soldiers on the field after battle. He used overlapping action during the famous homecoming scene and provided relief to break tension by comic bits, such as the forlorn sentry. An impressionistic ending again displayed Jesus Christ with the carnage of war.

The Birth of a Nation was too big to be financed by Mutual. A separate company, the Epoch Producing Corporation, was created in 1915 to finance and distribute the film. Harry Aitken, president of Epoch and the man who hired Griffith away from Biograph, was instrumental in the formation of Triangle Film Corporation. The new enterprise consisted of Griffith, Thomas Ince, and Mack Sennett, each a successful producer. Griffith supposedly supervised many films for Triangle,

[11] Ibid., p. 66 and Croy, op. cit., pp. 105–9.

but did not direct. He did, however, write eight original scenarios under the pseudonym "Granville Warwick" in 1915 and 1916. Griffith spent most of his time planning for *Intolerance,* which was to "out-spectacular" *The Birth of a Nation.*

The actors and directors at Triangle were all Griffith-trained, so it was no surprise to discover that *Hoodoo Ann,* directed by Lloyd Ingraham, possessed touches of the master. The film, released in 1916, starred Mae Marsh and Robert Harron and served as a prelude to their screen love affair in *Intolerance.* Griffith directed part of *Hoodoo Ann,*[12] which concerns an abused girl in an orphanage who saves another girl during a fire. Adopted by a wealthy couple, she is later courted by the neighbor boy who wants to be a cartoonist. In an incident, the girl thinks that she has killed the man next door, but he returns as she is about to confess to police. The orphan marries the cartoonist, who embarks upon a successful career.

The stars of *Hoodoo Ann* are introduced at the beginning with cuts to each, with an appropriate title. The iris was used to go into the girl's imagination. Cross-cutting between a film within this film and its two separate stories is effective and serves the same purpose as the cutting between a stage-play and the characters in the earlier *A Drunkard's Reformation.* Masking of the camera for a look into the closet and a tricky mirror shot demonstrated that Ingraham had captured his mentor's techniques. A tender bit of business transpires when the hero leaves the frame to kiss the girl and returns right afterward.

Profits from *The Birth of a Nation* were enormous. Griffith had no trouble in attracting investors, most of whom had financed Epoch, to back the Wark Producing Corporation. This separate organization was created to finance and distribute *Intolerance,* which opened at the Liberty Theater in New York September 5, 1916. Although the film received vast publicity and came on the heels of the successful *The Birth of a Nation,* it was a commercial failure. But as an artistic and creative venture, *Intolerance* may have been the most influential film ever made.

In his earlier achievements, Griffith hinted at the techniques he was to use in *Intolerance.* One sees the language of cinema used as few have ever employed it. The photography and its composition as well as all of the camera effects had been executed in *The Birth of a Nation;* *Intolerance* became a masterpiece at the editing table.

Griffith inter-cut four separate stories, linked only by a shot of Lillian Gish rocking a cradle and a quote from Whitman's *Leaves of Grass* —". . . endlessly rocks the cradle, Uniter of here and Hereafter." [13]

[12] Eileen Bowser, "An Annotated List of the Films of D. W. Griffith," in Barry, op. cit., p. 49.

[13] Ramsaye, op. cit., p. 756.

A modern story, "Christ in Judea," a medieval French Huguenot tale, and a Babylonian saga are presented side by side, with a fantastic climax featuring shorter and shorter cuts from each story. All but the modern one end in tragedy. *Intolerance* closes with a pacifist montage —prison walls become fields of flowers and battle-scenes change into strolling family groups.

Film-makers in later years not only copied *Intolerance*'s editing style but lifted many scenes. Eisenstein copied the factory workers' strike and the baby-spearing scenes; Pudovkin took the courtroom scenes. The tempo and rhythm of Griffith's instinctive use of short shots laid the foundation for the entire crop of Soviet directors while his impressionistic montages influenced the German school. Hollywood utilized Griffith's new concept of spectaculars interjected with sex in the films of Cecil B. De Mille.

Griffith used blue, red and yellow tinting for subliminal effects; for example, the cradle scene is blue and the society dance red. His characterizations of people and events in *Intolerance* can scarcely be described, and has been likened to plastically created photographed objects being dramatized by the camera "as though it were an individual spectator noting them in ensemble and then in detail, or vice versa." [14]

Early in 1917, before America's entry into World War I, Griffith reached the zenith of his fame. He was invited to England to make a propaganda film for the British government. *Hearts of the World* was made for Artcraft after his severance from Triangle. Starring Lillian and Dorothy Gish and Robert Harron, the film exploited anti-German feeling in the United States. It opened in New York on April 1, 1918, and was a commercial and propagandistic success.

Hearts of the World was shot in France, England, and California. It combined newsreel pictures, stock war footage, and recreated incidents. This eclecticism was used extensively a little over a decade later by the Nazi masters of propaganda. *Hearts of the World* opened with a newsreel shot of Griffith at the front, followed by a scene of him with Lloyd George at 10 Downing Street. Historical facsimiles developed in *The Birth of a Nation*, depicted "The Shadow" (the Kaiser in a sinister portrait), Churchill and Lloyd George waiting for news, the House of Commons, and the French Chamber of Deputies.

The story concerns two American families living in France in 1914. They are caught up in the German invasion. The boy goes to fight with the French to defend their common homeland, while the girl remains in a village subsequently occupied by German troops, who commit many atrocities. The French regain the town with the aid of the

[14] Parker Tyler, "The Film Sense and the Painting Sense," *The Three Faces of the Film* (New York: Thomas Yoseloff, 1960), pp. 44–45.

English and Americans. The Germans flee as the Americans parade in the village with the stars and stripes. The film closes on Woodrow Wilson's photograph draped with American flags.

Some of the more blatant propaganda scenes include children ravaged by war, the Huns whipping a French girl who cannot perform slave labor, and the obvious Wilson–American flag finish. One scene contrasts a bacchanal of German officers with the death of a French mother, victim of the war, and her burial by her sons. Another scene shows a girl walking alone on the battlefield after the fight, a scene that Eisenstein may have adapted consciously for *Alexander Nevsky*. *Hearts of the World* was considered highly effective propaganda in 1918.[15] Dorothy Gish as the quasi-streetwalker dubbed "The Little Disturber," was the highlight of the film, and her performance led to a brilliant career as star of a comedy series.

Another Griffith war film was *The Girl Who Stayed at Home* (March 23, 1919). Begun during the war and completed after, the film had no propaganda value. Pro- and anti-German elements mix ambivalently. One title describes a pro-Kaiser character—"Turnverein—half-drunk and half-German." The story deals with the granddaughter of a Confederate who had refused to surrender and now resides in France. Her fiancé, a French nobleman, is killed in the war, and she falls in love with an American fighting in France. A Hun attempts to rape her but a good German intervenes. The American has a young brother who returns to the U. S. to marry a Broadway showgirl loyal to him during the war. Griffith used limbo lighting for close-ups of the female stars. He employed some footage shot for *Hearts of the World*.

American movie-goers wanted to forget World War I. Griffith produced and directed several pastoral films for Artcraft in 1919. *True Heart Susie* featured a marvelous performance by Lillian Gish. Susie has put William through college secretly by selling her cow. He becomes a minister, but marries a "bad" girl. She dies, but he cannot marry Susie because of a mistaken vow. In time, he learns the truth and proposes. The plot sounds clichéd, but the acting and unassuming camera work combine to produce a delightful cameo of innocence. *True Heart Susie* opened in New York June 1, 1919, and included two touches that Hollywood would later make hackneyed: gauze in front of the camera lens for a daydream sequence, and the shadow of the boy at the window during a love scene, talking to the girl who is not in shadow.

While at Artcraft after World War I, Griffith commenced one of his "specials," *Broken Blossoms*. It was released May 13, 1919, by United Artists, a company Griffith had formed with Douglas Fairbanks, Mary

[15] Eileen Bowser, op. cit., p. 54.

Pickford, and Charles Chaplin. *Broken Blossoms* was an artistic and commercial success. Its narrative reflected the "Yellow Peril" fears prevalent at the turn of the century and even today. Griffith appeared to be trying to combat intolerance again, but with a "white man's burden" attitude. The alternate title of *Broken Blossoms* was *The Yellow Man and the Girl*. The illegitimate daughter of a villainous boxer is abused by him. A Chinese storekeeper treats her wounds and nurses her back to health. A spy tells her father, who smashes up the store and beats his daughter to death, whereupon the Chinese shoots the father and commits suicide. Lillian Gish and Richard Barthelmess starred.

Griffith, under controlled studio conditions of setting, lighting, and special effects, created a poetic image of Limehouse. His use of tinting for titles as well as different colorings for interior and exterior sequences, together with man-made fog, influenced the German studio films of the 1920s. The yellow tint for the Chinese-temple scene was striking. When Griffith showed the anger of Donald Crisp as the father, he cut from close-up to tight close-up to extreme close-up shots of the face. A scene of policemen reading a newspaper and exclaiming: "Better than last week, only 40,000 casualties," may have been a pacifist comment about World War I. In 1922, a "poor-man's" version of *Broken Blossoms* appeared with Lon Chaney starring in *Shadows*.[16] It proved that Griffith had already achieved what this film attempted.

In order to finance films for UA and to build himself a studio at Mamaroneck, New York, Griffith agreed to make three films for the First National Company. They were done hurriedly and lacked depth. First was a melodramatic potboiler, *The Greatest Question*, which opened in New York December 28, 1919. There are glimpses of primitive poetic symbolism, a technique that Dovzhenko was to bring to maturity a decade later,[17] e.g., Griffith cut from a shot of a dying mother to rushing water and back to the dying mother. Another example of such editing lyricism was a cut to the river from the lover's embrace and back again. Griffith inserted poetic titles among these shots but Dovzhenko let his images stand alone. *The Greatest Question* opens with a 180-degree pan to establish a rural locale. Defocusing of the camera was used for the revelation scene, as the girl remembered her past glimpse of a murder.

With these "quick and dirty" money-makers, Griffith introduced humor based upon stereotypes which he was to repeat in most of his speedily made films. When Griffith had time to create characteriza-

[16] *Broken Blossoms* was remade also as a sound film, in England, in 1935. Emlyn Williams took the role originally played by Richard Barthelmess.

[17] Arthur Knight, *The Liveliest Art* (New York: The New American Library, 1959), pp. 83–86.

tions, he seldom resorted to the one-dimensional stereotype. Zeke, the Negro servant in *The Greatest Question,* played by Tom Wilson in blackface, is portrayed as a liar and a thief. He eats at a separate table and possesses all of the "Uncle Tom" characteristics. As the picture ends and the poor family for whom Zeke works strikes it rich in oil, he enters in top hat and tails, with his dog bedecked in jewels.

Stereotypes of cannibals and natives appear in the second of Griffith's First National productions. *The Idol Dancer* (March 21, 1922) deals with a white trader and his half-breed daughter on a South Sea island. The savages are led by a renegade white "Blackbirder" in an attack upon the good Anglo-Saxons. Love scenes are extremely unsubtle. Aside from a typical last-minute rescue using cross-cutting, the film is distinguished only for its use of cutaways from the primitive island to civilized New York, a contrast effected without expository titles. Richard Barthelmess is telling the savage girl about the city, and there are cuts to the Third Avenue El and the Flatiron Building.

"No pushee-me good boy," is a line from Griffith's third First National film, *The Love Flower* (August 22, 1920). His conception of a South Sea native who is half-Black and half-Indian, with a Chinese accent, was probably shared by the majority of Americans. So, too, were his conceptions of the Afro-American. It may be therefore unjust to condemn Griffith for his screen renditions of social situations that reflected then current mores. Yet, when he did use the film for social protest, he did so with eloquence. The saving grace of *The Love Flower* was Griffith's visual impressions of moods, which were effective for the early 1920s. An example is a girl standing at the edge of the sea feeling the salt spray.

If while making these three potboilers Griffith was concurrently preparing and subsequently shooting *Way Down East,* then he can be excused for them. Shot on location in New England, *Way Down East* contains some of the most suspenseful sequences in motion picture history. The final ice-floe sequence is not artificial although spectacular, and it is exciting even today. The use of real ice, snow, and outdoor locations lends credibility to the melodramatic story. Pudovkin considered *Way Down East* a model of how background in a film can supplement and strengthen character and story.[18] For example, the climactic waterfall sequence is foreshadowed when the waterfall is seen earlier during a love scene.

From an antique stage melodrama for which screen rights cost $175,-000, *Way Down East* is mid-Victorian in plot but enriched with performance, atmosphere, and many filmic touches. In contrast to the three

[18] V. I. Pudovkin, *Film Technique,* translated by Ivor Montagu (London: George Newnes, Ltd., 1935), p. 129.

First National films, *Way Down East* required much time to make. Griffith used multiple camera angles and placements, including a moving sled. Technique was not new, but the shots of the gossip hurrying to spread the news about virtuous but pregnant Lillian Gish are extremely effective and give a sense of emergency and impending doom. Griffith once again used exit and reentry into the frame. Absence of the previous stereotypes give *Way Down East* its authenticity. Stereotypes were not needed because the characterizations are in depth.

In *Way Down East* a typically innocent girl is seduced by a cad, this time after a mock wedding. She gives birth alone in a cold New England boarding-house. The child dies but is baptized by the mother in a moving scene. She falls in love with an upright farmer who rescues her from an ice-floe just before it crashes over the falls. The storm scene was photographed during an actual blizzard in Mamaroneck and certainly must have influenced Pudovkin for his ice-floe sequence in *Mother*. *Way Down East* was released September 3, 1920, and was second only to *The Birth of a Nation* in its commercial success.

It is almost impossible to believe that *Dream Street*, released by UA April 12, 1921, was made by the same man. Sets from *Broken Blossoms* appeared to have been utilized, but *Dream Street* is overlong and poor. In this Yellow Peril film, a Chinese gambling king covets a dancer who tells him—"After this, you let white girls alone." In addition to the "Chink," a "Negro" is seen, for comic relief. Griffith attempted to incorporate a symbolic struggle between Good and Evil into the plot. A Gypsy violinist as Satan and a Street Preacher doing the Lord's work portray the combatants. Many scenes depict the characters being swayed, literally, in either direction. There are few effects worthy of mention. A fade-out was used not only instead of a dissolve but also in the middle of a sequence, as in the middle of an embrace. The camera was defocused as a man died. Gauze was used over the lens to create fog. An exciting use of the close-up to depict panic in a theatre was a hint that in a few years an Eisenstein could create the Odessa Steps montage. Griffith's cuts to hell and the Devil and then to Christ were repetitive of his early films.

Almost nine months later, the master returned with an old-fashioned, well-made spectacular (UA, December 28, 1921). *Orphans of the Storm* starred Lillian and Dorothy Gish as two orphans caught up in the French Revolution. The film contains two grandly suspenseful scenes: when Lillian Gish hears the singing of her blind kidnapped sister but cannot get to her, and the final big scene when Monte Blue as Danton saves her and her lover from the guillotine. Characters are two-dimensional, especially Robespierre as played by Sidney Herbert. Even Griffith made a brief appearance sipping champagne at a debauched soirée of aristocrats. The prologue of *Orphans of the Storm* compares the bloody events after the French Revolution to "present-day" Bolshevism. Titles refer to "Anarchy and Bolshevism of the Committee of Public Safety" and the "Revolutionary Government."

In *Orphans of the Storm* Griffith used a matched cut from a close-up of eyes to another close-up of eyes with the camera lens gauzed. For certain scenes, the camera was masked at top and bottom to give a wide-screen effect. At Versailles, the camera dollied back to give the feeling of spaciousness. When Louis XVI entered, Griffith panned the walls, reminding one of Resnais's *Last Year at Marienbad*.

One of the screen's early who-dunnits, *One Exciting Night* does not identify the murderer until its climax. Broadway actor Henry Hull portrayed the dashing young hero who wants to marry blackmailed Carol Dempster. Scotland Yard solves the case and the film ends on a bright note. A subplot featuring blackfaced Porter Strong as a comic Negro frightened by the mysterious events was not unusual for its day. Later, Negro actors were to replace white minstrel actors in such Hollywood mysteries of the thirties and forties as the Charlie Chan series, with its "funny" chauffeur, Mantan Moreland (who rolled his eyes "better" than Stepin Fetchit). Griffith's title during a tender scene: "Words cannot tell what he proposes in love"—is disappointing. A truly successful silent film made such descriptive titles unnecessary. *One Exciting Night,* released by UA October 2, 1922, lost money.

When Griffith left the studio and went out on location, he almost always produced a good film. *The White Rose,* which was opened in New York by UA May 21, 1923, was set in the bayous of Louisiana. A cynic might accuse Griffith of "arty" pictorialization, but the effect was that of a lovely postcard mailed from the Deep South. Mae Marsh stole the film as the girl seduced by a fallen minister. The scene with her using a discarded dog box for her baby is Griffith at his best. Later, Mae Marsh and her illegitimate child are harbored by friendly Negroes, servants of the minister's high-born fiancée. As Mae Marsh lies dying, the wealthy girl summons him. He discovers that this is the girl he had wronged, marries her, and he nurses mother and child like sick roses. A close-up of a rose closes the film.

Almost every schoolchild has seen footage from *America* (UA February 21, 1924). This spectacular was supposed to do for the War of Independence what *The Birth of a Nation* had done for the Civil War. It told the story of the American Revolution through two Colonial families, one Tory and one Rebel. Griffith exonerated the British for the war atrocities; instead the loyalists among the Americans are the culprits. In this story a Tory girl falls in love with a Rebel boy. She is rescued at the last minute from a British villain by a poor American farmer who had fought at Lexington and Concord. George Washington is portrayed as a Christ-like figure. He is shown in magnificent glory during Cornwallis's surrender. Washington is on a white horse, the camera faces the sun, which is blocked by the victorious General, giving him a terrific, shining glow.

America did not possess the believability of *The Birth of a Nation*. To Griffith's credit, he did not edit out the shot of Paul Revere's horse as it falls. This inclusion was the only believable part of the picture. No new techniques were used, although opening titles dissolve one to another.

Iris Barry has stated that Griffith's *Isn't Life Wonderful?* (December 24, 1924) "lacks the shock-value" of G. W. Pabst's *The Joyless Street*.[19] The former, shot on location in Germany in the summer of 1924, was made a year before its German counterpart. Yet it may have influenced Pabst[20] in his treatment of German post–World War I inflation. *Isn't Life Wonderful?* possesses a crisp semi-documentary style while the Pabst is a psychological interpretation. The latter may have more Freudian dynamite, but the Griffith contains the most subtle and remarkable images found in movies, according to James Agee.[21]

One of Griffith's finest chase scenes has the wounded war veteran and his fiancée running from thieves who finally steal their precious potatoes. Other outstanding sequences show people pushing on a meat-line as prices keep going up and the ripping of the Kaiser's picture by the Professor, who then kicks the pieces into a dust pan. A subjective shot of trees blowing in the wind, together with time-lapse photography of potatoes growing, mark the film as one of Griffith's most sophisticated ventures. Unfortunately, the irony of the title is missing from the story. Griffith's typical happy ending destroys the impact of the sullen existence of the characters. *Isn't Life Wonderful?* was Griffith's final silent film as an independent producer.

Griffith's first film for Paramount, which he joined as a staff director in 1925, was *Sally of the Sawdust*. It had no new or interesting film techniques. Comedy scenes were funny, due to the antics of W. C. Fields as a circus fakir who adopts an orphan. After many tribulations, some hilarious, the girl is united with wealthy relatives and Fields becomes a real estate agent. Griffith, in the closing title, compares this new occupation with the shell game and Fields' other circus gambling tricks.

The Sorrows of Satan came in 1926 for Paramount. Its street scenes and wedding shots are strictly Hollywood studio slickness, lacking any realism. The love scenes are very bad—nothing is left to the imagination. They are a far cry from the old Griffith, when characters delicately

[19] Iris Barry, op. cit., p. 32.
[20] Siegfried Kracauer, *From Caligari to Hitler* (New York: The Noonday Press, 1960), pp. 169–70.
[21] *Agee on Film*, edited by David Manning White (Boston: Beacon Press, 1964), p. 315.

stepped out of the frame for a kiss. The sole artistic touch is in the scene between Menjou as the Devil and Ricardo Cortez as the tempted one, when the pair walk in and out of pools of light. The Devil, of course, departs at the film's close because the hero repents. A final shot of Satan's "horrible" shadow vanishing is disappointing if one remembers Murnau's *Nosferatu* and its communication of terror four years earlier.

In 1927, Griffith signed with Joseph Schenck, the controlling force in UA, to work for Schenck's Art Cinema Corporation.[22] The master returned to Hollywood and made four films.

Drums of Love reunited Griffith with his old star from the Biograph days and *America*, Lionel Barrymore, who gave a brilliant performance as the hunchbacked Spanish nobleman whose handsome brother commits adultery with his young bride. The deformed giant kills his two beloveds at the close of the film. In an alternate ending the court jester kills Barrymore as the young lovers repent. Both finales are equally poor. The film contained several long moving camera shots, had some good action, and moved at a fairly rapid pace. Laboratory dissolves were used by Griffith for the first time. There is an effective subjective shot, from the brother's point of view, as he looks at the girl's body. The Art Cinema-UA release opened in New York January 24, 1928.

Griffith's first all-sound film (he had experimented with disc recordings previously) was *Abraham Lincoln*, starring Walter Huston, with a scenario by Stephen Vincent Benét. Typical of American history in the films of the 1920s, great Americans have no faults. It traces Lincoln from birth to assassination, emphasizing his well-known qualities. There is no dramatic continuity, plot, or sub-plot. Sound quality is poor and editing jumpy.

However, Griffith did use sound creatively. Off-camera sounds were utilized as well as sounds coming from the distance on long shots. The technique was similar to that of television drama in its early days. The camera dollied in on the person speaking, dollied out to a two-shot, widened for a group shot and came in on another person. Screen dialogue was not yet developed in 1930 when *Abraham Lincoln* was released by Art Cinema-UA, and there was a trace of stylized stage diction. Some scenes showed promise of a future film sound language, but Lincoln's monologues were mostly taken from his actual speeches and were wooden. Griffith was voted best director of 1930 for *Abraham Lincoln*, in spite of what Lewis Jacobs has called its "many moments of absurd sentimentality." [23]

[22] Eileen Bowser, op. cit., pp. 78–80.
[23] Lewis Jacobs, *The Rise of the American Film* (New York: Harcourt, Brace and Company, 1939), p. 394.

The Struggle was Griffith's last film, made as an independent and released December 10, 1931 by UA. It was withdrawn after unfavorable criticism. The story is the old-timer about the family man who becomes a drunkard. Griffith opens with a montage of conversations concerning alcohol. Street and steel-mill scenes are well directed and photographed. Hal Skelly, as the father, does an admirable job, especially in delirium tremens. His wife's line—"Jimmie, your eyes are all shiny"—is typical of the script. *The Struggle*'s good features are its realism and the quality of its sound track, the latter a tremendous improvement over *Abraham Lincoln*. Griffith reverted to stereotypes for humor in this quickly made film by inserting a Jewish bill collector into the story. If one were to criticize the happy ending, as the drunkard reforms and lives happily ever after, he should not forget the Academy Award-winning 1945 Billy Wilder film, *Lost Weedend*.

Sixteen years after *The Struggle*, Griffith died at the age of seventy-three. He had made 432 movies from 1908 to 1931, according to Agee, that had grossed $60 million.[24] Stern put the total number of films at a higher figure.

Aside from the huge gross of his life's output, Griffith's contributions to the art of the film are many. With Billy Bitzer, he enormously advanced the sophistication of the camera. He was a master editor. Screen acting in his hands moved ahead to far greater subtlety and expressiveness. Aside from many unforgettable individual characterizations, he provided spectacular scenes of great masses of people in action. He uplifted the taste of audiences and brought them from smelly, cheap nickelodeons to gilt palaces with huge screens and symphonic orchestras to provide accompaniment.

"A film," Griffith said, "is a cooperative effort between the director and the audience. A director shows a bit of human emotion; the audience fills in the rest. The better the film, the greater the cooperation between director and audience." [25]

Griffith at his peak let the content determine his film technique. His films integrated story, mood, title, and technique, blending schematically.[26] He may have carried Victorian morality long beyond its proper life-span,[27] but his themes of social consciousness are still valid. Although his recurring plots depicting the poor hero or orphan making good or the dire consequences of immorality or the evils of drink are unsophisticated by our contemporary existential non-standards, it can-

[24] *Agee on Film,* op. cit., p. 398.
[25] Homer Croy, op. cit., p. 75.
[26] Paul Goodman, "Film Chronicle: Griffith and the Technical Innovations," *Partisan Review* (May–June, 1941), pp. 237–40.
[27] Herb Sterne, "Screen and Stage," *Script* (January 8, 1944), pp. 12–13.

not be overlooked that these concepts still rest in the subconsciousness of the American people. So, too, Griffith's Southern fundamentalist religious view that Christ in Heaven is pitted against the Devil in Hell is believed by millions of persons.

One must take issue with Lewis Jacobs who claimed that Griffith was interested only in money and prestige, that he did not keep up with the times, and that as soon as the great director did not move forward, he disintegrated as an artist.[28] Griffith crumbled as a craftsman only when he did not have sufficient time to produce his films and when he could not retain overall supervision of the work in progress. As a Hollywood studio staff director, Griffith was as out of place in the twenties as Ingmar Bergman would be in Hollywood today. Griffith was indeed aware of his artistic successes. He did not bumble through his films as many have suggested.

In an interview with Ezra Goodman shortly before his death, Griffith linked *Intolerance* to *Potemkin* and to *Triumph of the Will*.[29] Such an astute observation could have been made only by a person well aware of the vast potentiality of the cinema, its relationship to history, and its impact on audience attitudes in the twentieth century.

[28] Lewis Jacobs, op. cit., pp. 384-94.
[29] Ezra Goodman, *The Fifty Year Decline and Fall of Hollywood* (New York: Simon and Schuster, 1961), p. 8.

David Wark Griffith: In Retrospect, 1965*

by G. CHARLES NIEMEYER, Ph.D.

Most film historians recognize that David Wark Griffith released, in 1916, the greatest moving picture that has ever been made or is ever likely to be made—so magnificent a masterpiece that its greatness was beyond the comprehension of most moviegoers, critics, and other film-makers in its day—yet a work which seen today, obviously takes its place beside Michelangelo's Sistine Ceiling, Shakespeare's *King Lear,* and Beethoven's Ninth Symphony! This film is *Intolerance.*

Furthermore, it can be seen that Griffith stands topmost among the geniuses who created and developed the new theatrical medium of the twentieth century—the cinema. Great innovations and great innovators in film art have been few; the basic line can be charted from Georges Méliès to Griffith, to Sergei M. Eisenstein, and on to Walt Disney. The great majority of film-makers, past and present, have been mainly followers and—for the most part, followers of Griffith.

BIO-FILMOGRAPHY IN BRIEF

Llewelyn Wark Griffith (1875–1948), who called himself "Lawrence" when playing on the stage and signed himself "David" as an author,

Originally published in Film Heritage, *vol. I, No. 1 (Fall 1965), 13–22. Reprinted by permission of Professor Niemeyer and* Film Heritage. *Professor Niemeyer has corrected and brought up to date the original article for publication in this volume. Dr. Niemeyer is Associate Professor in the Department of Speech and Dramatic Art at the University of Maryland.*

* Dedicated to William K. Everson in gratitude for immeasurable assistance in studying Griffith's films.

actually desired all of his life to become a successful writer more than anything else. First, the theatre and, later, the moving pictures were a means by which he hoped to achieve sufficient independence to realize this goal. His true life-ambition was never to be fulfilled.

Born on a farm at Crestwood in Oldham county, Kentucky, he was associated with newspaper work in Louisville from early youth and advanced from reporting to dramatic criticism. Soon he was acting with a number of stage companies while trying to establish himself as a poet, short-story writer, and dramatist.

Lack of sufficient regular work in the dramatic and journalistic worlds led him, while toying with Broadway, to sell film-stories and act before the moving picture cameras at the Edison and Biograph studios in New York. In 1908, at the latter organization, he was offered his first opportunity to direct a one-reel, 11-minute film: *The Adventures of Dollie.*

Since nothing more lucrative could be found and since he had become genuinely interested in the potentialities of movies, he continued at the American Mutoscope and Biograph Studios, 11 East 14th Street [in New York] and in Hollywood until 1913—by which time he had directed 494 shorts and the four-reel feature, *Judith of Bethulia,* released in 1914. During this period he did much to develop the grammar, syntax, and structure of the cinema beyond the primitive style of Méliès and his imitators.

Moving to the Mutual Film Corporation as production-head of the Reliance-Majestic Studios in 1913, he supervised a number of features but actually directed only four—all of which he authored as well: *The Battle of the Sexes* (1914), *Home, Sweet Home* (1914), *The Escape* (1914), and *The Avenging Conscience* (1914).

At the same time, he was making *The Birth of a Nation* (1915), which began as a Mutual production but, ultimately, became so expensive that it was independently financed and released under the Epoch Producing Corporation. With this picture he achieved still greater development of cinema grammar and further complexity of structure —proving himself to be the greatest world-genius in films to that time.

In 1915 he joined the Triangle Film Corporation to serve also as a production-head, but he actually devoted most of his time to *Intolerance* (1916), which also became so expensive that it was independently released by the Wark Producing Corporation. This film still represents the utmost complexity and elaboration of both grammar and structure ever achieved in any moving picture, and it has schooled film-makers throughout the world for decades. Unfortunately, it was so advanced and above the heads of the populace that it incurred a tremendous financial loss; this D. W. took upon himself to protect his investors, carrying the burden through the 1920's until he had paid all debts, to the extent of nearly a million dollars.[1]

In 1917 he moved to Artcraft Pictures—later to become Paramount Studios—and began *Hearts of the World* (1918), also destined to become an independently released work. Other Artcraft films directed by him were: *The Great Love* (1918), *The Greatest Thing in Life* (1918), *A Romance of Happy Valley* (1919), *The Girl Who Stayed at Home* (1919), *True Heart Susie* (1919), and *Scarlet Days* (1919).

Broken Blossoms (1919) began as an Artcraft film but ended as Griffith's first release for United Artists Corporation, which he, Douglas Fairbanks, Charles Chaplin, and Mary Pickford organized to distribute their own creations.

In an effort to reimburse the stockholders of the Wark Producing Corporation for the tremendous loss on *Intolerance*, he edited that picture into two smaller films which were released as: *The Fall of Babylon* (1919) and *The Mother and the Law* (1919).

Moving to his own studios at Mamaroneck, New York, in the same year, he began a series for release by First National Pictures: *The Greatest Question* (1919), *The Idol Dancer* (1920), and *The Love Flower* (1920).

Creations for United Artists followed: *Way Down East* (1920), *Dream Street* (1921), *Orphans of the Storm* (1921), *One Exciting Night* (1922), *The White Rose* (1923), *America* (1924), and *Isn't Life Wonderful* (1924).

His own studios soon proved too costly, and he was obliged to abandon them, moving to Paramount Pictures to replace Cecil B. De Mille, who—disgusted with conditions at Paramount—was departing to his own studios.

It was not long before D. W. also said farewell to Paramount in similar disgust after directing: *Sally of the Sawdust* (1925), *That Royle Girl* (1926), and *The Sorrows of Satan* (1926), which latter film De Mille had wished to make.

Signing with Art Cinema Corporation, he completed four more films for United Artists release: *Drums of Love* (1928), *The Battle of the Sexes* (1928), *Lady of the Pavements* (1929), and the sound-picture, *Abraham Lincoln* (1930).

In 1931—in the midst of the Depression and Hollywood's chaos over the coming of sound—both DeMille and Griffith, along with many

[1] Seymour Stern estimates that the total cost of *Intolerance* was two million dollars. He states also that had it been made in 1936 it would have cost ten to twelve million. "An Index to the Creative Work of David Wark Griffith. Part II: The Art Triumphant (c) *Intolerance*," *Special Supplement to Sight and Sound*, Index Series No. 8 (September, 1946), pp. 15–16.

others, were jobless and extremely uncertain of their futures. In a sudden, frantic effort to grasp at straws Griffith made *The Struggle* (1931) independently.

Thereafter, he devoted himself to literary projects, a radio program, and a film at Hal Roach Studios, *One Million B.C.* (1940), which should not be considered among his works, inasmuch as he withdrew his name from it. He spent his last years closeted alone in his hotel room—trying to shut out the world—so he might concentrate on realizing the unfulfilled career of David Wark Griffith—author.

THE ECLIPSE OF HIS REPUTATION AND THE TRAGIC NEGLECT OF HIS WORK

Today the name of D. W. Griffith is totally unknown to the average student graduating from our American universities. The typical man-in-the-street, under the age of fifty, has never heard of him. There are a few from both groups who have heard of a picture called *The Birth of a Nation,* but they do not associate it with any artist-creator. Only a handful of these have actually seen the film in any form.

The number of Americans who can list six masterworks of Griffith is infinitesimal; and only a few scholars can name thirteen more of his feature-films which are of artistic and historical significance.

Yet fifty years ago, *The Birth of a Nation* was a raging subject of conversation from the White House to the lowliest barroom; and for ten years afterward David Wark Griffith was renowned throughout the world as the leading master of moving pictures.

The failure of the United States to honor sufficiently the memory of Griffith and recognize the greatness of his work is a heinous crime, which generations to come will ultimately set right. It is as if Walt Whitman, or Emerson, or Thoreau, or Poe—any great, native creative artist had been interred with his creations.

The body of his work was monumental. From 1908 to 1913 he directed 494 short pictures, predominantly one-reel 6–12–15 minutes) in length and, from 1911 on, he also made two-reelers.

Beginning with his first multi-reel feature in 1913 he continued to explore the possibilities of this form through the entire "golden age" of the silent film into the sound era and completed his 35th such film in 1931.

Out of a total of 529 pictures, 345 now survive and others may be discovered: 315 short films, some from every year (1908–13), and 30 features (1913–31). This constitutes an almost year-by-year documentation of the development of cinema art during the first four decades of the century—a gold mine of primary source material for ages to come. It is unfortunate that but few teachers of film can presently even begin to deal adequately with the artist and his work. There is no worthy biography nor reliable and thorough study of his contribution. A few, out-of-date, critical essays—full of errors of fact and judgement —have been employed as sources repeatedly, until what is currently available in English—for the most part—amounts to sacrilege.

A major reason for this state of affairs is that the academic world, from primary school on to university, has been unduly backward in recognizing the moving picture as worthwhile creative art—in the same sense as literature, music and painting. Furthermore, it is just dawning on our American consciousness that films can be just as permanently a part of our cultural heritage as books, symphonies, and landscapes.

As moving-picture directors come to be regarded as artists in the United States, their body of works will become associated with their names precisely as the plays of Shakespeare, the quartets of Beethoven, and the pictures of Van Gogh are related to their creators. Griffith's star will one day rise high again in the firmament, where it belongs.

NEW YORK CITY'S MUSEUM OF MODERN ART PRESENTS A SECOND RETROSPECTIVE EXHIBITION OF HIS FILMS

The Museum of Modern Art Film Library, 11 West 53rd Street, in New York City has done more than anyone else to preserve, circulate, and present public exhibitions of Griffith's films. After rescuing deteriorating prints by paying delinquent storage fees, they brought Griffith and his famed cameraman, G. W. "Billy" Bitzer, to their vaults to aid in the restoration of as many pictures as possible. By exchanging prints with other American and foreign archives, several curators have worked over many years to salvage and make his creations a permanent heritage; and the work is still in progress.

The Museum has held two retrospective exhibitions of his pictures for the public at large—the first, in 1940, with D. W. himself in attendance—and the second, from April 25 to July 31, 1965. The latter endeavored to present the greatest number of his films ever seen at such an event: 42—16 early shorts and 26 features—plus two others with which he was associated. The event commemorated the fiftieth anniversary of his most famous picture, *The Birth of a Nation* (1915) .

The screenings were planned to include 17 films that have become available since the 1940 exhibition—7 of which have not been seen publicly since their original release. However, the restoration of *Lady of the Pavements* (1929) had not been completed by the end of the festival and *The Battle of the Sexes* (1928) was not received from Paris as scheduled; these two will be exhibited in the near future.[2]

Mrs. Eileen Bowser, Assistant Curator[3]—who supervised the entire project—issued a new edition of the Iris Barry work: *D. W. Griffith: American Film Master,* with many new illustrations and fifty additional pages of text, attempting to formulate the most complete filmography in print with the fullest assemblage of credits for the features. This is the most valuable single book on Griffith's entire work to reach publication, but future editions should remove the errors which appear.

In the gallery outside the film auditorium was displayed a notable selection of stills from both shorts and features with a number of production shots and portraits of Griffith. Another outstanding highlight was the piano accompaniment of all the silent films by Music Director Arthur Kleiner, who played from original filmscores in the Museum's collection as often as possible. The pictures were screened at soundspeed which gave them a lively pace and a suitable dramatic flow.

This event was one of the most notable and distinguished of its kind ever given and met with such hearty public response that seats were in quite short supply for the greatest and most renowned pictures.

Although many of the film-goers were unfamiliar with the players and the archaic acting style in the older works and did laugh from time to time, there was almost always exuberant applause at the conclusion of a bill.

The greatest enthusiasm was stirred by the screening of two, original, tinted prints—that of *Intolerance* (1916) and of *Broken Blossoms* (1919). Despite the fact that these films were known to many in black and white versions, the color generated the sensation of actually seeing these pictures for the first time! Spontaneous applause broke out from time to time during the glorious unrolling of *Intolerance.* It is tragic, indeed, to realize that when these two original prints perish, as they will soon, the world will know only the pictures shorn of their

---

[2] *Lady of the Pavements* was screened October 20–24, 1965, and proved to be one of Griffith's top secondary works. In the author's opinion, it ranks second to the best film of that year, Ernst Lubitsch's *The Love Parade.* Griffith's work is his most sophisticated effort and shows him to be both a student and master of the "Lubitsch touch."

The Battle of the Sexes has never been screened by the Museum despite the author's continuous pleas since 1965; nor has the Museum obtained a print of this work. A letter from Associate Curator, Mrs. Eileen Bowser, dated August 7, 1970 states: "Unfortunately, we won't be able to get THE BATTLE OF THE SEXES in the near future," and refers the author to a print at George Eastman House. William K. Everson considers this film to belong with Griffith's unsuccessful works.

[3] Associate Curator at the time of revising the original article, August, 1970.

magnificent color.[4] This has already happened to *Judith of Bethulia* (1914), *The Birth of a Nation* (1915), and several later features.

A second remarkable aspect of the festival was that it restored to the screen the greater part of the careers of many renowned actors, who are now either deceased or in retirement. Lillian Gish emerged as the greatest actress of the silent screen, magnificent in both tragedy and comedy. Uniquely, she is still active, having spent the summer playing Shakespeare at Stratford, Connecticut.

Mae Marsh was second in the hearts of the audience and Carol Dempster beautifully and precisely achieved the effects D. W. desired. Among males, Richard Barthelmess in juvenile leads was preeminent, followed by Robert Harron and Neil Hamilton. In more profound roles H. B. Walthall, Lionel Barrymore, Walter Huston, and Donald Crisp were most impressive. One great comedian delighted with his drolleries—W. C. Fields. In addition, there were many fine performances by faithful minor players who served as members of Griffith's stock company.

The short one and two-reelers, which Griffith ground out at a rate averaging two a week, for more than five years, are quaint little items vividly bringing back the spell of nickelodeon programs, as well as the melodramatic histrionics of the popular stage.

The opening bill of these shorts brilliantly demonstrated D. W.'s gradual elaboration of the "last-minute-rescue" from the crude format of Edwin S. Porter's *Rescued from an Eagle's Nest* (1907)—in which Griffith plays the lead—on through *The Lonely Villa* (1909), *The Lonedale Operator* (1911), and *The Girl and Her Trust* (1912). Here it is possible to see embryonic development of the superlative final sequences of *The Birth of a Nation* and *Intolerance*.

Many of these, turned out in a day or two, were indeed crude and naive. Griffith had a very exhausting schedule and was able to concentrate on only an occasional "favorite," bringing to these superior artistic treatment in every detail.

The best of the shorts seen here was his second two-reel effort, *Enoch Arden* (1911). Wilfred Lucas plays Enoch; Frank Grandin, Philip; Griffith's wife—Linda Arvidson, Annie Lee; and Enoch's small son is Robert Harron—the Biograph property-boy, who later developed into one of D. W.'s favorite juvenile leads.

Since this film was made before two-reel pictures had been accepted

---

[4] Mrs. Eileen Bowser informs the author that new safety, tinted prints of both films have been acquired recently by the Museum. These were realized by an Eastmancolor inter-negative process under the guidance of Don Malkames. The Museum hopes that within a few years they will be able to circulate similar colored prints in 16 mm.

by exhibitors, the first reel was shown on the Monday bill and the
second on the Thursday program; Mondays and Thursdays were always the best days at the nickelodeons because of D. W.'s films. Before
his name was known and used to promote his pictures, special signs
were set out before the film theatres announcing "Biograph Night."

An Attempt to Rank His Features on the Basis of Artistic Achievement

The opportunity to see twenty-six of Griffith's features in chronological order provides an unusual perspective both on the highest peak of
the director's career and on the general developmental trends of the
film through the so-called "golden-age" of the 1920's. For the first time
it is possible to evaluate the whole quality of his work, to see its relationship to that of his contemporaries, and to compare it with that of
his many successors through three-and-a-half decades. Many new, important critical judgements can be made.

First emerges the fact that at least six pictures may be considered
masterpieces, not only of their own day but for the present and future
as well. Such a judgment is based on the subject-matter and ideology
as well as on cinematic treatment—which would include: film structure
and organization, use of grammar, quality and effectiveness of the
acting, and general artistic level of designing, camerawork, editing, and
auxiliary details. In sum, the over-all level of directional skill, imagination, and creativeness.

These six appear in order of achievement: *Intolerance* (1916),
Broken Blossoms (1919), *The Birth of a Nation* (1915), *America*
(1924), *Orphans of the Storm* (1921), and *Abraham Lincoln* (1930). All
these still pack a terrific wallop to ordinary spectators who have no
critical lingo except "digging."

To allay fires of controversy it is wise to explain why *The Birth of a
Nation* is in third, rather than second place. The fact must be faced
that this picture, when it was first made, was, and still is—*satanic* in its
subject-matter! It aroused a tremendous wave of both praise and condemnation: praise for its cinematic magnificence—condemnation for
its theme of savage intolerance of the American Negro.

In brief, it glorifies criminal persecution, deprivation of the vote,
brutality, and murder by the Ku Klux Klan. It is so vicious in arousing
white sex-jealousy and fear that one contemporary college student, on
seeing it for the first time, said: "It makes me want to go out and kill
the first Negro I see!" During the 1920's the Ku Klux Klan screened the
film extensively in the Mid-West to build up a vast membership and
succeeded; it is potent and savage propaganda.

For long years after the attack on Griffith for this production he sought in many films to atone for this intolerance. Both *Intolerance* and *Broken Blossoms,* beside being unique in film history, are on the side of the angels. *America, Orphans of the Storm,* and *Abraham Lincoln* are also on the same side, but artistically they are each just a bit short of Satan's field-day.

Thirteen secondary pictures are yet entertaining for both a popular or critical audience and are all well-made "programmers"—except for the early epic, *Judith of Bethulia.* D. W., who frequently said that making pictures was more of a business than an art, always differentiated between his well-made "sausages" and his great art-works. Although loving the art of great films, he was aware that solvency was primarily based on popular successes. DeMille and others have continually reflected this same, practical artistic ambivalence in professional film-making.

The top secondary works may be ranked in order of excellence: *Sally of the Sawdust* (1925), *Lady of the Pavements* (1929), *The White Rose* (1923), *Way Down East* (1920), *The Sorrows of Satan* (1926), *The Idol Dancer* (1920), *The Girl Who Stayed at Home* (1919), *Drums of Love* (1928), *The Love Flower* (1920), *True Heart Susie* (1919), *The Avenging Conscience* (1914), *A Romance of Happy Valley* (1919),[5] and *Judith of Bethulia* (1914).

The nine features unmentioned seem unsuccessful for a variety of reasons, although several are quite ambitious efforts. They are given in chronological order, since it is unprofitable to measure degrees of weakness: *Home Sweet Home* (1914), *Hearts of the World* (1918), *Scarlet Days* (1919),[6] *The Greatest Question* (1919), *Dream Street* (1921), *One Exciting Night* (1922), *Isn't Life Wonderful* (1924), *The Battle of the Sexes* (1928), *and The Struggle* (1931). Two others, *The Fall of Babylon* (1919) and *The Mother and the Law* (1919), fall into no man's land— being, actually, fragments of *Intolerance* and seeming weak out of context.[7]

The ranking of 30 films in order of artistic excellence may seem foolhearty, since no two average spectators or Griffith-specialists would agree 100 per-cent. But with such a guide never ventured before, teachers and critics have been utterly at a loss to ascertain which works might fall into the categories: great, good, and bad. This effort at such a classification is presented here in the spirit of sheer deering-do.[8]

[5] Acquired by the Museum in 1968 and ranked by William K. Everson as being somewhat below *True Heart Susie.*

[6] Acquired by the Museum in 1968 and ranked by William K. Everson as being among Griffith's unsuccessful works.

[7] The final two films have been seen by the author since the 1965 retrospective.

[8] This ranking of Griffith's films does not include the features: *The Battle of the Sexes* (1914), *The Escape* (1914), *The Great Love* (1918), *The Greatest Thing in Life* (1918), and *That Royle Girl* (1926), which Professor Niemeyer was unable to evaluate since no prints of these films are known to exist.

RE-EVALUATION AND CRITICAL INTERPRETATION: HIS POSITION TODAY

From this remarkable retrospective exhibition and some consideration of the rest, which was not seen, emerges an understanding which
prompts a re-evaluation, such as is only possible after time has passed
and dust settled.

In sheer bulk of pictures directed and film-footage released, Griffith
has never been surpassed by anyone. Other directors have made more
features: John Ford, 132, Henry King near 100, Maurice Tourneur
about 75, and Ernst Lubitsch about 71. The greatest record for short
films before and concurrent with D. W. was that of George Méliès,
who made approximately 542. Griffith's major contemporaries, Thomas
Ince and Mack Sennett, were primarily production-supervisors—directing much less than they administered over other directors, as has been
equally true of Walt Disney.

Because of the size of his creative output and the world fame of his
greatest films, Griffith's influence is still predominate in the structure,
grammar, and syntax of the contemporary moving picture. Major directors, who know his work first-hand, constantly acknowledge that
almost nothing has been added since his time.

Television from its inception aped and mimicked the grammar and
structure of the cinema, which it found ideal for its own needs. Twenty
years later, film and film style are still dominant. Consequently, if
D. W. should ever glimpse a monitor from his spiritual vantage point,
he will be sure to say, "Why I did all that long ago at Biograph!"

Griffith also towered over all his predecessors and contemporaries in
the high purpose with which he approached film-making. In the earliest
days, when nearly everyone else was grinding out low-grade melodrama
and farce, he strove to make as many films of a higher type as was possible, drawing stories and themes from literary classics, biography, and
history.

Inspired by the social criticism in the plays of Henrik Ibsen and the
novels of Frank Norris and buttressed by his strong Christian outlook,
he lashed out against injustice, abuse, corruption, and other evils. A
strong fervor, a sincere patriotism, and a high-minded idealism were
almost constantly present in his work—occasionally, even to excess.

To the end, it was his aim to employ the new art-form, which he had
done so much to develop, as an educative force within the frame of
entertainment. Even the satanic presence in *The Birth of a Nation*
was an effort to reveal what he felt to be the actual and insufficiently
disclosed truth about his victimized Confederate ancestry.

In his idealism he was also a poet with a ceaseless passion to create
cinematic beauty. From the first days he sought ideal locations, at-

mospheric lighting effects, and pulchritude in the persons of his actors. This endless quest for beautiful effects of every kind was part of his romanticism and continued to increase as his style developed. He also delighted in depicting beauty of character as often as possible—glorifying nobility, moral purity, chivalry, maternal love, good breeding and graceful manners. Since the majority of these things are today largely out of fashion, they seem a quaint affectation to modern eyes.

It is true that he was sentimental to a great degree, but this was a radiation of his own loving-kindness—comparable to Albert Schweitzer's "reverence for life," Robert J. Flaherty's camera caressing the universe, and Walt Whitman's eternally embracing arms. D. W. was fond of idealized romantic love, handsome loving couples, attractive children, radiant family-groups, animal pets, roses, and glowing sweeps of landscape.

In the much harsher modern age this romanticism seems sugary and old-fashioned. Today the mode is rather for slum squalor, human bestiality, dull and literal depiction of the ordinary, every-day humdrum, and exploration of naked human flesh in search of erotic excitation. In his later years he detested the films then current for having lost the concept of the beautiful and the poetic.

But for all of his true sentiment he was fully aware of the savage nihilism rampant in life, the terror of tragedy, the wrack of human suffering, and he portrayed these with an honesty and courage that has not been surpassed or often equalled. Seeing the whole of existence, he sought to evoke joy and gratitude for the presence of so much beauty, continuing to repeat, "Isn't life wonderful?"

Being so very great in so many ways, he was also vulnerable with many weaknesses. Bred in the age when romanticism luxuriated in the theatre and melodrama stalked the boards, he was never fully able to rise above the many clichés which served as staple stuff in the Biograph period. He adored the novels of Dickens, where both sentimentality and melodrama still ride rampant.

Never ceasing to believe that he was himself the best scenarist in existence and constantly burning to prove himself a great author, he too often wrote his own scripts, under a variety of fancy plumes. The result was that many films repeated the old stereotypes mechanically, lacking a sense of reality and becoming all too much alike.

He was an amazing farm-boy in infinite ways, but he was never truly able to achieve sophistication nor over-ride the stubborn Fundamentalism in his religious upbringing. His serious devotion to idealism and sentiment so pervaded his personality that he was slow in developing a strong, balancing sense of comedy and wit.[9]

[9] *Sally of the Sawdust* and *Lady of the Pavements* reveal his comic sense at its artistic height.

His career floundered at a time when almost all the heads in Hollywood were toppling, and he was not alone in failing to re-establish himself in the bedlam of the sound-era. However, there is absolutely no evidence whatever to indicate that his artistic skill or judgement deteriorated throughout the "golden-age" of the 1920's, as Lewis Jacobs has emphasized [10] and endless others have repeated without knowledge. Griffith followed every style and type of film which seemed the vogue and succeeded artistically, if not commercially, with the best of his confreres. But all of the topmost directors, during this hectic period, did suffer both artistic and financial failure with some regularity.

Who has equalled Griffith in the decades since *Orphans of the Storm* (1921), *America* (1924), and *Abraham Lincoln* (1930)? Sergei M. Eisenstein was schooled by his earlier masterworks and made notable achievements both in the silent and sound ages, but he left no such body of work as Griffith and none to equal *Intolerance*. Cecil B. DeMille took over D. W.'s mantle in the sound age, pouring forth mammoth and spectacular pageants, but only his last film, *The Ten Commandments* (1956), may be rated near to Griffith's best.

Ernst Lubitsch rode high from silent days through many successes and failures in sound; but he—like our current Hitchcock—admitted he only manufactured toys to please moppets.

On the recent scene loom Stanley Kramer, Elia Kazan, and Vittorio De Sica, who possess a near-match of Griffith's social consciousness and moral fervor, but none approaches D. W. in cinematic imagination or screen poetry.

Ingmar Bergman and David Lean, on the contrary, are nearer to D. W. in this exotic quality, but have no particular social awareness.[11]

In retrospect, David Wark Griffith still appears to be the giant of his day and of 1965 as well. The question will be asked for decades to come, "When will we see his like again?"

[10] Lewis Jacobs, *The Rise of the American Film* (New York: Harcourt, Brace and Company, 1939), pp. 384–94.

[11] Bergman's films, *Winter Light* (*Nattvardsgästerna*—1962) and *Shame* (*Skammen* —1968) are notable exceptions.

The contribution of Carl Theodor Dreyer (1889–1968) is not related to that of Griffith because it is currently in the process of being re-evaluated. In recent critical studies Dreyer's films have been considered to be seriously flawed from *The President* (1920) to *Gertrud* (1964). *La Passion de Jeanne d'Arc* (1928) has been called one of the most controversial silent films ever made and has been totally damned by Ado Kyrou in his *Le Surréalisme au Cinéma*, 1963. Dreyer's subsequent works have also met severe critical reception by international reviewers. See Ebbe Neergaard, *Carl Dreyer: A Film Director's Work*, translated by Marianne Helwig, New Index Series No. 1 (London: The British Film Institute, 1950), and Eileen Bowser, *The Films of Carl Dreyer* (New York: The Museum of Modern Art, 1964).

Griffith the Man

by LILLIAN GISH

He was a good, loving son, brother, and uncle. He had been deeply attached to his mother, whom he had supported until she died, a short time after Dorothy [Gish, Lillian's sister] and I came to work for him. I dimly remember his going back to Kentucky for her funeral. He also helped support most of the other members of his family. Among his papers, I found letters asking him for a new house or a new car; seldom was there a notation saying, "We saw your picture and enjoyed it." But he would never admit that people used him. I suppose he needed to be needed—and he was, by literally hundreds of people.

I believe one of the reasons that he felt so close to us was that we never asked him for anything. Consequently, he seemed to trust us more than he did most people.

His generosity extended to all who worked with him. "Sometimes he would call for extras to report, knowing full well that his shooting schedule precluded their use," Mack Sennett once said. "But it was his way of seeing that actors made a few dollars." At other times he would invite the extras to lunch with him. "He must have felt a good solid meal now and then would be welcomed," Sennett suggested. "He was once a hungry actor himself."

Whenever I knew of an actor who needed a job, I would ask Mr. Griffith to use him—and he always did. Ray Klune, who started with him as an office boy, finished high school and went on to college with Mr. Griffith's help.

He turned no one away. If anyone asked for a handout, Mr. Griffith would put his hand in his pocket, and whatever bill he came up with

—a five, a ten, sometimes a twenty—he would hand over. If someone
had a problem that could not be solved with cash, Mr. Griffith would
ask one of his assistants to look after the person and help him.

When a projectionist ran film at night, he was paid for it. But, in
addition, Mr. Griffith would pull a bill from his pocket, slip it into
his hand, and thank him. It was usually $10 but often could be $20.
He always expected to pay for what he wanted. He gave out of pride,
mingled with appreciation.

Mae Marsh[1] told me that he once paid the funeral expenses for a
deaf little Italian voice teacher, though he had never met the man.
She had told him how the neighbors were trying to take a collection
and couldn't raise enough, so he asked her mother to attend to the
arrangements, then paid for them.

One of his gifts to me was a fiery opal from Australia, which he
had made up in a pendant. He himself never wore jewelry, except
a ring with an Egyptian stone that Harriet Quimby, a woman flier
and a friend of his, had given him. The ring could be used as a seal,
to stamp letters, and also as a weapon. It could inflict injury in a
fight.

Yet he could be inconsistent about money. I remember his making
us take care of his tips, claiming he had no change. Years later, he
would saunter through the rooms of my house in Beverly Hills, casually emptying the contents of all the cigarette boxes into his pockets.

"She has more money than I have, because she's working," he would
say. "And besides, she doesn't smoke."

It amused him to pretend to be a pinchpenny. Once Mary Pickford
told me that sometimes when he took her and her mother to dinner,
he would say that he had no money on him, but that the Pickfords
were so rich it couldn't matter to them if they paid the bill. So they
always came prepared. He did it as a joke and they knew it and
laughed at it.

Gift giving was one of his few extravagances. Mr. Griffith never
wanted more than one or two rooms in a middle-class hotel, and
never owned a house until late in his life, when he married Evelyn
Baldwin and they bought a tiny house on Peck Drive in Beverly Hills.
He ate and drank sparingly; I never saw him drink more than one
glass of beer or one whiskey and soda with dinner. He always advised
us to eat nourishing food but not to overeat. He often told me that
I was the only one who didn't eat too much, although he knew of my
weakness for ice cream.

He did smoke a good deal, however, although he never carried
cigarettes. He would call out, "Give me a cigarette," and every man

[1] [One of DWG's leading ladies; she played Flora in *The Birth of a Nation* and
The Girl in the Modern Story of *Intolerance*.]

in the room would hold out a pack. He would look over the assortment and choose the brand he wanted. Then there would be a flurry of lighted matches. It was considered a great honor to have one's cigarette chosen. He would take a few puffs on the cigarette and then throw it away.

He had a great regard for his body and believed in keeping it healthy. He boxed every morning. Mack Sennett said that he also took a cold bath each morning, adding pails of chipped ice, delivered by the bellhop, to his bath water. He was very frightened of germs. He always worried about catching cold, perhaps because it was the only illness he seemed to know. The only times that I remember his actually being ill were when he had colds. He took great precautions against them. If you had a cold, you weren't allowed near him. He always kept doors closed and avoided drafts, particularly in automobiles. He didn't like having colds because, although they never stopped him from working, they made work an effort. When he had one, he would complain and swear about it, but he was never absent from work because of illness in all the years that I was with him.

His preoccupation with keeping fit was a concern with which I was particularly sympathetic. As a child I had been delicate and undernourished, but I had had a strong will to survive. I soon learned that in our profession if you were sick or tired, you simply kept quiet about it and did your work. To stand the strain of a fourteen-hour day six or seven days a week, you had to be in top physical condition. If a performer looked pale or run down, Mr. Griffith was apt to pass him by. I don't know how he happened to accept me, for I was the picture of frailty. Perhaps my work in the East Fourteenth Street studio had convinced him that I was hardy. Perhaps he was reassured because I was always on time, never complained of late hours, and never showed a sign of illness. The quality I had cultivated as a child on the road—what my friend Nell Dorr calls "Lillian's blinders"—helped me. I always concentrated on the job at hand and shut out everything else from my consciousness.

Once I brought a young girl, Lucille Langhanke, to Mr. Griffith's attention. She wanted to break into pictures, and I persuaded him to let me film a test of her. Afterward he explained to her in his courtly manner that there were no openings. But he told me privately: "She's beautiful but far too delicate. I don't believe she could stand the grind."

It's possible, however, that he was simply annoyed because I exposed over 1,000 feet of film testing Lucille. "Who do you think you are?" he demanded when he saw the test. Whatever the reason, Lucille didn't brood. Soon after, she became an outstanding player and changed her name to Mary Astor.

Mr. Griffith had almost a mania for cleanliness. He himself was always impeccably groomed, and he expected the young actresses on the lot to be equally immaculate. A female aspirant would lose out if she weren't scrupulously clean. Once, after an interview with a talented actress whom he had dismissed, he said exasperatedly, "She just doesn't *look* clean."

One morning Dorothy appeared at the studio wearing blue jeans, with her hair in kid curlers. He spoke to Mother about it, and Dorothy never repeated her mistake.

Mr. Griffith's emphasis on hygiene once had an unexpected consequence. Dorothy had been assigned to play the role of Kathy in *Old Heidelberg* [1915].[2] Her leading man was Wallace Reid, who was much older than she. John Emerson, an important man in the New York theater, was to direct it as his first film. When they were about to film the first love scene, he told Wallace to kiss Dorothy on the mouth.

"Oh, Mr. Emerson," she exclaimed. "We don't do such things in pictures."

"You're going to do it in this picture," Emerson said ominously. "How else are you going to play a love scene?"

"In films," she informed him, "we pretend to kiss. And with the camera at a distance, it seems that we do."

"Well, this time the camera is close and I want you to kiss him."

Not Dorothy. She turned and rushed off for "Daddy" Woods' office, with John Emerson in hot pursuit. Frank Woods, a kindly, white-haired man whom we all called "Daddy" Woods, was not only head of the story department but also judge in all our disputes.

"You know Mr. Griffith told us we must *never* kiss actors—it isn't healthy," she complained to him. "But Mr. Emerson doesn't seem to understand."

Mr. Emerson was furious. "How can I do a love story without a love scene?" he yelled.

The whole studio was interested in the dispute; it became a *cause célèbre*. Wally's wife heard about it. She called Mother and told her indignantly that her husband was perfectly healthy and that it certainly would not hurt Dorothy to kiss him. Finally Mr. Emerson won, and a tearful, rebellious Dorothy kissed Wallace Reid on the mouth before the camera.

D. W. Griffith was a proud man. We who knew him saw his pride as the pride of achievement. Strangers, to whom Mr. Griffith was an enigma, tended to misinterpret this trait as vanity.

Although he was reputed to be vain, he lacked the conceit to con-

---

[2] [DWG produced the film, in which Erich von Stroheim played his first significant role.]

sider himself more than a director. Even later, when he wrote the stories for his twelve-reel films, such as *Hearts of the World* [1918], he used a pseudonym. He held no exaggerated idea of his own importance. Unlike many American producers, he never criticized the European directors and producers. He had the highest regard for the Italians' camerawork, though he thought they lagged behind Americans in the telling of a story. He claimed later that America progressed faster in film making because of a four-year head start, during the time Europe was embroiled in World War I.

In going through his papers recently, I was startled to discover that he considered himself ugly. The truth is that he was striking and distinguished-looking. But apparently his failure as a leading man had confirmed his poor opinion of his looks. Looking back, I realize how much the size of his nose embarrassed him. At that time he avoided being photographed and seldom appeared in a newsreel. He did allow himself to be seen in films like *1776, or The Hessian Renegades* [1909], perhaps because he considered the costume sufficient disguise.

He was in the habit of wearing wide-brimmed hats, not only for protection from the sun on location but also because he believed that they balanced his jutting nose and strong chin. But someone had warned him that hats were bad for the scalp, so he sliced off the tops in the hope that the sun's rays would halt the thinning of his hair. He used to sit, watching the filming, one leg crossed over the other knee, and unconsciously massage the top of his head. If there was a wind and his headgear felt insecure, he would calmly thread a shoelace through the brim and tie the ends together in a neat knot under his chin. But he affected none of the idiosyncrasies of the directors who made breeches and puttees symbols of the Hollywood director.

There was a suggestion of mystery about Mr. Griffith that has never been solved. He admired and loved women, yet he seemed afraid of them. He never saw a girl in his office without a third person present. He seemed concerned about his reputation. Perhaps he was simply protecting himself from blackmail. Hollywood was already filled with ambitious girls who would stop at nothing to get into films. Some unscrupulous young girls, having obtained an interview with a producer, would threaten to remove their clothes and accuse him of rape if he didn't promise them a role in a movie.

Mr. Griffith worried about the reputation of his youthful actresses as well, and sometimes lectured them on the dangers of venereal disease. "Women aren't made for promiscuity," he warned us. "If you're going to be promiscuous, you'll end up having some disease."

One of the films he made for Mutual was Paul Armstrong's sensa-

tional drama *The Escape* [1914], which had to do with the horrors of
syphilis. It was a daring topic for its time, and he handled it with
power and taste. It was a better sermon for his innocent young actresses
than any warning he could utter.

It was impossible to be neutral about Mr. Griffith. Like all men
of great stature, he inspired both admiration and dislike. His secretary Agnes Wiener, who probably knew him as well as anyone did,
thought that the reason Mr. Griffith was considered "odd" and
"lonely" was that he was an intellectual giant among a tribe of
pygmies. He had a vast knowledge of literature and music. Agnes told
me that there were more than 1,000 classical records in his suite at
the Alexandria Hotel.

But, if he seemed unlikable to those who did not know him, he
inspired absolute devotion in the members of his company. In later
years Billy Bitzer [DWG's cameraman] always said, "The happiest
period of my whole life was my sixteen years with Mr. Griffith." We
young actresses especially adored him, and he returned our affection.
He enjoyed our company. Mae Marsh once told me:

"My first trip to New York—the 'Big City,' as he called it—I was
to see all its wonders, and he arranged small parties to enjoy it with
me. One Sunday, he took Gertrude Bambrick [one-time dance director
for DWG], Eddie Dillion [film actor and occasional director], and me
to Coney Island, and what a fine time we had!

"Although D. W. was much older than many of the young boys I
dated in New York or California, he could sometimes act like a child.
Once we took a hansom cab through Central Park. We were both
singing at the top of our lungs when we were stopped by a policeman
on horseback. He looked into the cab and asked, 'Lady, you all right?'

" 'Yes, officer,' I said. 'We are just rehearsing for the Met.' "

Often when we were filming outdoors, Mr. Griffith would take any
of the young girls who happened to be nearby for a walk and point
out nature's beauty.

"Some Sundays," Mae recalled, "when he didn't have anything better to do, he would drop by at our house for dinner, which my mother
usually served midafternoon. After dinner, we would take a walk
through the woods, which were at the top of the street, and, after
resting a while and listening to the very interesting things he would
talk about, we would have a foot race. D. W. almost always won."

He would often take us to the theater, especially the Yiddish
theater and the Italian theater. He admired all the ethnic theaters,
and we learned from them all.

Mr. Griffith disliked eating alone. He had a habit of moving around during a break in rehearsals and whispering to a select few, "Let's have lunch at Luchow's" or "Let's have dinner at the Astor." He loved his little secrets, and he would quietly invite a few members of the cast to a meal with the air of a medieval conspirator.

Mae Marsh told me, "Gertie Bambrick and I soon discovered that if we were late in taking off our makeup—while he was watching the previous day's rushes—then we all would be meeting at the front door of the studio, and he would ask us to dinner, sometimes alone but mostly with other actors, who also managed to linger behind and be included in the invitation."

Occasionally he would gather a group who liked to dance and would take us all to the Ship's Cafe in Hollywood for an evening of fun. Charlie Chaplin was often there with his own party, which always included an attractive girl. Mr. Griffith was by then a good dancer and never stopped until the music ceased or an early Sunday-morning call sent him home for sleep. Of all exercise he loved dancing most. There was rivalry among both men and women over who would be invited for these evenings.

It is easy to understand why Mr. Griffith inspired such enthusiasm in his staff. He had a commanding voice and a dramatic way with words. He was a great storyteller, and when he started to talk people would gather round; then he would start to shadow-box, and we all knew it was time to go back to work.

Yet for all his warmth and good spirits there was an air about him that forbade intimacy. In all the years that I worked with him I never called him anything but Mr. Griffith, and he called me Miss Lillian or Miss Gish. Although there was never any resemblance to a formal atmosphere in his studio, only with Billy Bitzer and Joe Aller [DWG's photographic lab director] did he relax enough to use first names. Dozens of times during the day we could hear his deep voice calling, "Billy, Billy!"

Even after Dorothy and I left Mr. Griffith, a certain formality remained with us. When Dorothy returned to the theater in the Depression years, she found it difficult to call the director by his first name, although she knew him well.

At the end of two weeks he said, "You don't like me, do you?"

"I don't know where you got that idea," she replied. "I do like you —very much."

"But you never call me by my first name."

"That's the way we were brought up," she explained.

"Mr. Griffith had an air about him that commanded respect," Mack Sennett recalled once. "Most of us called him Mr. Griffith. It seemed right that way. It was only after knowing him a couple of years that

I began to call him D. W." Off the set Mr. Griffith kept pretty much to himself and never discussed his private affairs. "He was an extremely difficult man to know."

Yet he could be quite emotional. One night during our first summer with him, he took Dorothy and me to a New York restaurant. After dinner, as we were leaving, the orchestra began to play a sentimental tune of the day. He hummed softly in his beautiful voice, and his eyes misted over. He was so virile and robust that I would never have imagined that he could be touched so easily. But he was—and often, I later learned.

If an actor did a scene well, Mr. Griffith would hug him and say, often with tears in his eyes, "That's a darb!" "Darb" was one of his favorite words, though rather out of place in his usual flow of rhetoric.

After a hard, tense day, D. W. would find relaxation in quoting poetry or prose appropriate to the mood of the scenes that had just been filmed. Sometimes when a child was in a scene, he would pick the youngster up in his arms afterward and talk to him. He was good with children, and they adored him. He could get more from children than any director I've ever known. If he wanted them to cry, they cried. He would show them what he wanted and stimulate their imaginations.

He was unfailingly kind and sensitive, never more so than when he was auditioning actors. A Griffith tryout was comparable to one in the theater, tense and difficult both for those participating and for those watching. Mr. Griffith would talk to the actor, coach him, try to make him feel at ease. If the actor failed, Mr. Griffith was always gentle and tactful in dismissing him. He had known too much failure himself ever to reject anyone brutally.

Billy Bitzer wrote that in all their years together he never saw Mr. Griffith in a real temper more than a half-dozen times. If someone displeased him, he would reprove him in a gentle voice. He might say, "What were you thinking of?" and then pause. His gentle manner was more effective than anger. The culprit usually did better afterward.

Although he was unusually patient, he could get angry, and I learned to stay out of his way when an explosion took place. But there was often humor in his anger. I once heard him express his reaction to a well-known Broadway producer: "I've always had a rule in life that I don't discuss a bastard I don't like."

Once his temper was set off when a bit player wanted to leave the set on some trivial pretext. In that period each scene was shot just once, and Mr. Griffith gave the fellow three minutes to change his mind and stay. Mr. Griffith took out his watch and timed him. The man charged at Mr. Griffith, who defended himself and knocked the fellow out cold.

Mack Sennett once told some of the company what happened on location one day, when Sennett was still an actor.

"One of the actors began to use foul language. The Boss' southern blood came to a boil, and he told the man to cut it out because there were ladies present. The actor told Mr. Griffith to go to hell. One word led to another, and soon they were slugging it out, toe to toe. The fight never reached a decision because others on the set pulled them apart. But it gave all of us new respect for Griffith. We knew he was man enough to back up his opinions with his fists, if need be."

In general, Mr. Griffith avoided violence. If he had problems on the set, particularly on location, where strangers watched and sometimes caused trouble, he would behave with great courtesy. If his attitude was not enough to control the situation, he would draw a bill from his pocket and pay the fellow to leave.

"I wouldn't give him a dime," Billy once protested.

"The delay is costing us more than I gave him," Mr. Griffith replied.

Once, while his actors were changing into their costumes in an empty shack, a stranger came up to Mr. Griffith and said; "You the boss man?"

Mr. Griffith, anticipating trouble, pulled $5 from his roll and handed it to the man, asking at the same time, "Does this shack belong to you?"

"Oh, no, sir," the man answered. "I was just wonderin' how to get a job."

Billy often told friends that he thought Mr. Griffith believed that money could buy whatever he needed to make the filming go smoothly.

Although he always maintained his authority, Mr. Griffith was not above assisting with the physical labor that is often involved in film making. When the manual laborers had to build a shack for a set, Mr. Griffith would not be found on the sidelines supervising. He would pitch in and work beside the men with pick and shovel, even on a hot day. He made them feel that he wouldn't ask them to do what he wouldn't do himself. When he stopped, he would say, "You know, it makes you feel a whale of a lot cooler when you stop after a bit of exertion on a sultry day like this." Then he would hand a shovel to an actor standing nearby and say, "That's really so—try it." And soon all the men of the company would be helping.

Above all, Mr. Griffith was a film maker. Nothing came before his work. The people in his life had to conform to his style of living, which was dictated by his overriding purpose—to create films.

Agnes Wiener said that she had to be prepared to take dictation at any time of day or night. "I've taken notes on the backs of theater programs, paper sacks, newspapers, and napkins."

He usually signaled that a speech was coming on by saying: "Got a pencil? I want to dictate."

"I think," Agnes added, "that dictation was largely a means whereby he could organize his thoughts. After he dictated, I typed them up, double-spaced, and gave the notes to him. He never seemed to make use of the material. Just left it lying around until it disappeared."

One day he sent Agnes to the bank. He said, "They'll give you $4,000."

Agnes had never seen so much cash at one time. She slipped him the roll of bills, which he put in his pocket.

"Aren't you going to count it?" she asked.

"Haven't got time," he answered, going into the next room. A second later he peered back at her. "But I will—next time."

One morning he arrived on the lot, well-dressed as always, but wearing one brown shoe and one black shoe. It made him seem less Olympian to us but also revealed that his mind was always on his projects. He had a habit of walking away from whomever he happened to be talking to, as if his mind were still on the work he had left.

He let no one hamper the realization of his visions. As I came to know Billy Bitzer better, I found that he didn't seem to take anything seriously. He was jolly and easygoing even in the midst of pressures—an amusing relief for Mr. Griffith. But often he would balk at Mr. Griffith's suggestions. Mr. Griffith, however, always obtained what he wanted in the end. He would see a scene in his mind and ask Billy to translate it.

"But that's impossible, Mr. Griffith."

"Then we'll do it."

Mr. Griffith might want both the horses in the forefront and the people in the distance in focus. Billy would tell him that it couldn't be done. But Mr. Griffith would insist, and he would get the shot.

He was a zealot of a new and uncorrupted art. "Do you know," he would tell us, "we are playing to the world! What we film tomorrow will stir the hearts of the world—and they will understand what we're saying. We've gone beyond Babel, beyond words. We've found a universal language—a power that can make men brothers and end war forever. Remember that. Remember that, when you stand in front of a camera!"

To us, Mr. Griffith was the movie industry. It had been born in his head.

Fade-Out

by LILLIAN GISH

The night that *Uncle Vanya*[1] ended its engagement at the Biltmore on November 29, 1930, D. W. Griffith came backstage to congratulate me. I hadn't seen him in quite some time. It was more than eighteen years since that midsummer day when Mother, Dorothy [Gish], and I had entered the old Biograph Studio. He made no mention of his plans; his departure from the payroll of United Artists had made his future a question mark. He talked mainly about the D. W. Griffith Corporation, which had been set up in his name in 1920 to sell stock to the public. He told me: "These are people who saw and loved my pictures and because they believed in them, they have invested all their savings. Hard-working men. Widows with children. How can I let them down? It keeps me awake at night, trying to figure out which story will make money."

In March 1931, when Dorothy was playing in Shaw's *Getting Married,* she received a note by messenger.

"Dear Dorothy," she read, "I bet you won't do this. I bet you won't come over and have supper with me at the Astor Hotel after your performance."

It was signed "D. W. Griffith."

Dorothy thought that it was some kind of college prank. Nevertheless, after the show she went to the Astor. D. W. was in an alcoholic stupor; he had probably been drinking when he sent the note. There was a nurse in the room trying to take care of him.

It made Dorothy ill to see what was happening to this great man. It seemed that there was no longer any place for him. He could not

From *Lillian Gish: The Movies, Mr. Griffith, and Me* by Lillian Gish with Ann Pinchot (Englewood Cliffs, N.J.: Prentice-Hall, Inc., 1969), pp. 313–16. Copyright © 1969 by Lillian Gish and Ann Pinchot. All rights reserved. Reprinted by permission of Lucy Kroll Agency and Prentice-Hall, Inc. Title and footnote supplied.

[1] [Lillian Gish played Helena in this production by Jed Harris.]

make movies the Hollywood way, which meant that he could not make movies at all anymore. The enforced leisure, to say nothing of the blow to his pride, must have been unbearable for a man who had worked so hard all his life.

Then D. W. seemed to regain control of himself for a while. He came to our apartment for dinner one night in the spring. With his usual secretiveness, he spoke guardedly of a film that he was planning, another talkie. From what we could tell, it seemed to be concerned with the problems of alcoholism. We made the logical deduction that it drew on his own experiences and did not pry. Actually, the story was based on a novel by Émile Zola, *The Drunkard*. D. W. did not tell us where he was getting the money, but evidently he had been awarded a fair-sized tax refund two years earlier, and the company treasurer had invested it in stock. In spite of the Depression, the stock made money and that, plus a small bank loan, was enough to finance a low-budget picture.

Paramount agreed to let him use one of its sound studios. A small cast was assembled, and rehearsals began. But at the last minute the dealings with Paramount fell through. Mr. Griffith scouted frantically for a place to work and finally rented the studio in the Bronx where in 1913 he had shot the interiors for *Judith of Bethulia*. I heard that he was working with second-rate equipment, forced to shoot some scenes outdoors, where the primitive sound equipment could not pick up the actors' voices. He labored through the film. *The Struggle* opened at the Rivoli in New York on December 10, 1931, and the reviews were dreadful. One trade paper bypassed a review out of respect for Mr. Griffith's former stature. He hid in his hotel room and refused to see anyone. *The Struggle* ran for one week, and then United Artists withdrew it from general release.

It was the last film D. W. Griffith ever made.

The Film Library of the Museum of Modern Art ran it recently for Anita Loos and me. Anita, who wrote the script with her husband John Emerson, had wanted to treat the story humorously, with Jimmy Durante in the leading role. It seemed to her the only way that the film could turn out well. D. W. seemed to give her suggestion serious thought, but in the end he filmed it as a drama, with Hal Skelly in the lead and Zita Johann as his wife. Except for a certain vividness in the factory sequences, where Mr. Griffith showed his usual skill with documentary scenes, I was disappointed with the film and saddened by his attempt to copy himself.

When D. W. Griffith stopped making movies, the purpose went out of his life. He was the hardest-working man I have ever known. During the years I worked for him, he spent sixteen hours a day and sometimes more on the job, with never a vacation. Intense, driving work insulated him from the world. In the beginning, his creative talent was nourished by exposure to the people in his company. But success and fame put him on a pedestal. He became surrounded by men who bowed to his orders when what he needed was the friction of independent minds. It is a sad fact that one must suspect those who say, "You're wonderful." It seems to me that one should count all one's critics as friends.

He also lost touch with the common man, whom he had loved and with whom, particularly in his early years, he had felt a close kinship. He isolated himself in a remote studio. He built his own little world of work at Orienta Point and left it only for increasingly unpleasant trips into the other world, either to find money or to fight censorship. He stayed at his studio all day and then watched rushes until 1:00 or 2:00 in the morning. He lived in a small house on the estate and ate his meals in the commissary. Once his chauffeur said to Agnes Wiener [DWG's secretary]: "What is the matter with the Boss? Has he no family to see?" Sadly, although he helped to support many members of his family, he had none.

When he had to go to work for other people to obtain money, his films suffered. He needed artistic control to make successful pictures. He failed completely whenever he deliberately set out to make a commercial movie; he did not understand what audiences of the time required and could not believe in the films he was doing.

His good friend Herb Sterne once said to me, "D. W. made the virginal the vogue, and it reigned until Volstead, gin, and F. Scott Fitzgerald gave birth to the flapper." His concept of woman was shaped by his inheritance and environment. The line of demarcation was sharp between the good girl and the girl whose morals were elastic. I remember when we reported to Mr. Griffith that Marguerite Clark, in her first film, *Wildflower,* had taken off her stockings right before the viewer. He was shocked.

"Doing such things before the camera!" he exclaimed. "How can I compete with that?"

He was also shocked when in *Joan, the Woman,* made before Joan of Arc was canonized, Cecil B. De Mille added love scenes to her story. And he was appalled at the way that the Bible was transferred to the screen. "I'll never use the Bible as a chance to undress a woman!" he said.

He saw himself as similar to a newspaper editor, in a position to affect not only his country but also the world. He regarded his films as the news, editorial pages, features, human interest, comics—and he took an editor's responsibility for his point of view.

Some of his strengths were also his failings. He believed that he was the heart, mind, and soul of his movies. He was right about the director's role, but being right did not always bring commercial success.

He made a serious mistake in not capitalizing on the success of the players he created. He believed that whom he used in a film did not matter as much as the story itself and how it was told. He seemed confident always that if he lost one fine actor he would discover another equally good. Yet often, in the midst of production, he would suddenly regret the loss of a favorite player. "Why did I ever let Dick go?" he would say. "He would have been perfect in this!"

Some time after the failure of *The Struggle,* the D. W. Griffith Corporation went into bankruptcy. At the auction that followed, D. W. was the highest bidder for the rights to twenty-one of his films. He bought them for $500.

Tribute to the Master
by ERICH VON STROHEIM

I have been asked to talk about D. W. Griffith because I have worked for four years under him, and was at one time his first assistant. I've been asked to concentrate whatever I might have to say into approximately fifteen minutes—fifteen hours wouldn't be enough to start.

Four years of close proximity and personal contact with Griffith gave me the opportunity to know that great man better than most of those who have worked for him. For those few, I hope, who do not know who D. W. Griffith was, I may say he was the pioneer of filmdom; he was the man who made the first great motion pictures—*The Birth of a Nation, Intolerance, Broken Blossoms, Way Down East, Hearts of the World*, to name only a few. He was the first man who had put beauty and poetry into a cheap and tawdry sort of amusement which some people had shamefacedly accepted while waiting for a train or to seek shelter from the inclemencies of the weather. He was the man who invented the close-up, to give to the poor man the same intimate view of the interesting subject in the film as the rich man derived from looking through his opera glasses at whatever interested him on the legitimate stage, with that difference, of course, that Griffith decided what the man in the box as well as the one in Nigger Heaven was to see at close range, and when.

The close-up of a person was to emphasize, at a given moment in a play, that person's thoughts, his expression and his reaction, as the close-up of an inanimate object accentuated its dramatic importance. Griffith was the man who invented it. The money men, as well as the exhibitors, thought Griffith had gone crazy; the latter refused at first to show these stupid torsos. Who would want to watch human beings without legs? The movement was the main objective; the thought, the meteoric

From Peter Noble, Hollywood Scapegoat: The Biography of Erich von Stroheim (*London: The Fortune Press, 1950*). *Copyright 1950 by Peter Noble and reprinted with his permission. Stroheim's tribute is the text of a broadcast he recorded in Paris and was originally broadcast December 30, 1948.*

power behind that movement was unessential. Today, almost fifty years later, his close-up is constantly and successfully used in almost every film. He was the first man who fully realized the potentialities of the motion picture. It was he who had made motion pictures the most popular and influential medium of entertainment the world has ever known. His films were the first to draw the intelligentsia to the theatre; it was Griffith who first realized fully the extraordinary opportunity the motion picture afforded for the making of propaganda. It was he who made the first and most important film for the Allied cause in the First World War, *Hearts of the World*. It was in this film that I acted as Mr. Griffith's first and personal assistant and military expert, besides playing the part of the German officer.

I had been working under Griffith since 1914, but when Griffith went to France in 1917 after the entry of the United States into the war, I had lost my job and I was stranded in New York. It was winter, and very cold. I had pawned my overcoat, and my only blue serge suit was awfully shiny at the elbows and at the seat. I ate once in a while on the borrowed meal ticket of an actor friend. In that same restaurant I had made the acquaintance of a kindly old doctor by the name of Ralk. We used to have long and learned conversations. One night I was extremely depressed. This doctor informed me that he had just read about the return of D. W. Griffith from France and England, and that he was scheduled to make a great propaganda film for the Allies. Knowing that I had previously worked for Griffith, he asked me whether I wasn't going to see my former boss and offer my services. Being as depressed as I was, disheartened, I refused, but the little doctor did not accept my "no" for an answer. At the end of the evening he demanded that I'd be in his office the next day at two o'clock.

I had decided not to go because I felt that there would be no use, and I would only make myself small in the eyes of the man whom I adored, but nevertheless, at two o'clock I found myself in Dr. Ralk's office. He ordered me to take my coat off, rolled up my sleeve, and without answering my questions, he gave me a shot in the arm. What it was that he had injected, I never did find out, but whatever it was it worked. For months I hadn't dared to look at any woman because I knew I looked so shabby, and it gave me an inferiority complex, but when I crossed the street to go to Griffith's office, I noticed a beautiful blonde coming in the opposite direction. I looked at her with what I thought were devilish eyes, even turned around after her and scrutinized the shape of her legs; I realized that the doctor's injection had done something to me. I reached Griffith's office, but was stopped by an over-officious office boy. Not paying any attention to him, I simply vaulted the balustrade, went direct to Griffith's private office. His deep voice asked me to enter.

I made the best click and bow I have ever made in my life. He seemed very glad to see me. After the preliminaries, he asked me what I was getting these days, meaning what salary I was demanding. "For you, Mr. Griffith, I work for a ham sandwich a day." There was a slight pause. "You are leaving tonight for Los Angeles." That was the way Dr. Ralk's injection worked, and that is the way I became once more Griffith's assistant. What that film *Hearts of the World* did for the Allies has never been justly appreciated; it caused hundreds of thousands of men and women of more or less pro-German audiences in the United States to have a complete change of heart, and the Teutonic arrogance and brutality exposed in that film caused many a man to enlist in the Army. It was Griffith who first realized the necessity of music, and especially mood-setting music as accompaniment to films, and it was he himself who composed most of the stirring music of his films.

It was Griffith who first felt the sacred duty to show everything, may it be sets, costumes, uniforms, customs or rituals, as correctly as humanly possible, even at that early stage when it was not so easy to conform with actuality as it is nowadays.

It was he who fully realized the education values of the film and felt personally responsible for the authenticity of everything in them. It was D. W. Griffith who first and fully realized the psychological effect of a proper and correct costume on the actor. It was he who insisted, for instance, on a real consecrated pyx being in the hand of the prison chaplain who accompanies Robert Harron to the gallows in the famous film *Escape*. That actor, carrying that pyx, felt as much a priest as if ordained. It was D. W. who invited famous stage stars of that time, to contribute their histrionic ability to films for the betterment of that entertainment—Sir Herbert Beerbohm Tree, Constance Collier, Douglas Fairbanks, to mention only three.

It was Griffith who, through this move, put the motion picture on the same level with the best productions of the legitimate stage. If Griffith had not been the greatest motion-picture director of all times, he could have been a great poet, a great commander of armies perhaps —perhaps even a Pope. But without doubt, great in any endeavor. If you live in France, for instance, and you have written one good book, or painted one good picture, or directed one outstanding film, fifty years ago, and nothing ever since, you are still recognized as an artist, and honored accordingly. People take their hats off and call you *maître*. They do not forget. In Hollywood—in Hollywood, you're as good as your last picture. If you didn't have one in production within the last three months, you're forgotten, no matter what you have achieved ere this. It is that terrific, unfortunately necessary, egotism in the make-up of the people who make the cinema, it is the continuous en-

deavor for recognition, that continuous struggle for survival and for
supremacy, among the newcomers, that relegates the old-timers to the
ashcan.

D. W. did not have a last picture, not of late. The last one he did
have, had not turned out so well. The producer who sponsored that
opus had misgivings from the beginning. Griffith was in financial stress
when friends engineered this undertaking for him. In the past, Griffith
had been too great to beg, too independent for the film financiers,
but this time they were determined to outwit him. They had the story
all ready, his shooting-script all ready, the sets all ready—everything
was ready. They were afraid that the great master would overstep, in
his imperious way, their schedule and their budget. Griffith's heart had
been almost broken by his previous bitter experience, so the ungrate-
fulness and selfishness of their campaign made him lose heart completely. Lesser men were afraid that the master's method might be out
of date, so they gave him new blood to put in what the new times demanded. He, the man who had written all of his film stories himself in
his mind only, because Griffith never used one page of script in all his
films, was to megaphone a story with which he had nothing to do
personally. So to say, a metal hamburger, preconceived, prearranged,
and almost predigested. Griffith did what he could in the circumstances,
just to fulfil his contractual obligations. But naturally, it was not a
success, not worthy of a Griffith.

So the greatest man the cinema had, or will ever have, died practically poor and a forgotten man. He died in the heart of the most
heartless town in the world—Hollywood. He passed away mourned
only by those few who had the chance to work for him, no matter in
what menial capacity that might have been. In 1914, I had the honor
of sweeping his stages at the old barns on Prospect Avenue in Hollywood which served as the Reliance Majestic studio. In short order I
became extra man, a Hollywood term for supernumerary, played bits,
worked myself up to small parts, and the eyes of D. W. fell on me. I
was engaged as assistant director to John Emerson, a former famous
stage director under the personal auspices of Griffith.

In 1917, as I said before, when Griffith returned from the front in
France, where he had been induced to make a propaganda film for the
Allied cause, he selected me as his personal first assistant. It was this
great film, *Hearts of the World,* in which I also played the German
officer. In that capacity of Griffith's assistant and actor I had the opportunity to become personally acquainted with the man Griffith. I've
met thousands and thousands of people in my life, but I have yet to
meet an equal to D. W. His enemies, and there were many, called him
"Hook-nose Dave." Tall, always slender, even with advancing years,
with those sharply hewn features, the aquiline nose, the nearly bald

pate, the overprominent lower lip, and wrapped in a white toga he could have magnificently impersonated a Roman senator. Paradoxically this finely-constructed, sensitive, aesthetic man, who has given the world the first film poetry, this sculptor of everlasting and outstanding screen characters had a deplorable penchant for loud, check, almost county suits and overcoats, and ever-so-broadly striped silk shirts, and floppy panama hats of gigantic size. But had he had overalls on, he would have attracted everyone's attention because he had what we call "allure." His walk was of a majestic cadence. I have never seen him to hurry. He never drove a car himself.

Perhaps it was the former actor in him that made him behave as he did, that made him do and say things as he did, realizing that a hundred eyes were always watching him, and that a hundred ears were listening. His voice was deep and mellow, and he spoke slowly with pauses between each word, as if he were in search for them. All his disciples tried to ape him as much as they could, some of us achieving a second-rate imitation of his voice and his utterances. Some of us, those who had enough money, sported striped shirts, a few even crowned themselves with panamas. Never once, even at nerve-straining moments during battle scenes, with earth-shaking explosions roaring around him have I heard Griffith raise his voice. Even his imperious command to cut was said in a low voice, only understandable to his assistants, who then repeated it so that the masses could hear.

Never have I heard him use a swear word or any vulgar expression so frequent in the vocabulary of motion-picture directors. Never have I seen him in anger, at least never outwardly, and, heaven knows there were many occasions for him to be angry, even with me.

As all great men, he surrounded himself with capable personnel. I was one of them, men who worked for him day and night with little sleep and little food, with little money, for months and months, not because he made them work like that, but because they wanted to.

To be working for D. W. Griffith at that time was the top, the topmost honor that could be possibly conferred upon anyone in Hollywood. It meant prestige. It meant the chance around the corner; it meant everything to me.

There was nothing small in that man's make-up. Even the smallest thing took on dimensions. Generous to a fault, he died poor, as it behoves an artist. I happened to know that once, I think it was in 1923, he had a deposit of thirty-seven thousand dollars in the safe of the Alexandria Hotel in Los Angeles where he had lived for years. Four years later, they found the deposit and notified Griffith. He had forgotten all about it. Not that he had so much money that he could afford to forget that amount—no. But money meant little to him, unless it was to spend it in great style; he never gave less than a five-dollar gold piece as a tip, even for the smallest service rendered. Of course that was in that good old time when we all got paid in gold (in California at least) and when Griffith was at his height.

But even when he had to battle for his existence, he was always over-generous. The type of woman he loved was the ethereal type, like Lillian Gish. He loved to dance; I believe that is what kept him young. Griffith was not a man to inspire intimacy. There was always a certain distance between him and his employees and coworkers, which he, with all his kindness and human understanding, knew how to preserve without becoming snobbish.

One can imagine how I felt when he visited me in 1941, twenty-five years after I had left his service, in my little shabby dressing room in the theatre in Philadelphia where I played in *Arsenic and Old Lace,* during my tour through the United States. My role was very exacting, physically at least, and I perspired freely. I was just getting a rub down after the last act when the door opened and D. W. entered.

He kissed me on both cheeks. I have received quite a few honors in my life, but that kiss of the master was the highest honor that could be bestowed on me. So long, Master, so long, D. W.

The Art and Death
of D. W. Griffith

by JAY LEYDA

The occasion was unpleasant, rather than tragic. The man who lay in the coffin had not been without bitterness and irony, both in his life and work, but even he could not have matched the irony of his own funeral services. As often as he had heard himself criticized as sentimental, no pale heroine of his molding had ever flaunted the false sentiment of this "memorial service." The floral tributes were rearranged for the photographers. The boys' choir hired for the ceremony giggled and rehearsed its dirge. Most of those arriving, however, were too busy contemplating themselves to be offended—we had outlived him, some of us (the latest to arrive) had done much better for ourselves, we might even do a little job-hunting so as not to waste the afternoon. The social arbiter at the door, recognizing and seating only those great who were still collecting weekly checks, ignored some of the men and women who had been the closest and most valued associates of the great man. A former actress of his, now a newspaper columnist, wore a more restrained hat than usual—as her tribute. When the expected number of the "respectable" didn't show up, the hall was opened to the filling flood of the curious who waited outside for the coming and going of celebrities. The occasion was not elevated by the first speaker; his "last respects" to David Wark Griffith struck a polite note of regret.

But then, toward the close of the second speech, the atmosphere changed. Donald Crisp, an actor whose firm position within the film industry has never wavered, began to speak of his friend, whose position had not only wavered, but crumbled:

From The Sewanee Review, *LVII (1949), 350–56. Copyright 1949 by Jay Leyda and* The Sewanee Review *and reprinted with their permission.*

It was the tragedy of his later years that his active, brilliant mind was given no chance to participate in the advancement of the industry. Difficult as it might have been for him to have played a subordinate role, I do not believe that the fault was entirely his own. I cannot help feeling that there should always have been a place for him and his talents in motion pictures. . . .

And then it happened. Someone sobbed inarticulately—it sounded like "Yes, yes—why not?"—and this one note of genuine emotion overturned the passive insincerity of the occasion. When Mr. Crisp continued, his voice, too, broke; "Our responsibility to these pioneers of our industry should go beyond the simple necessities of a room and board. . . ." By the time the pain of his prepared speech came to an end, the emotions of speaker and the audience were loosed and real. Then the efficiency of the "memorial" took over again, and the boys' choir, singing "Abide with Me," drowned out the sobs.

Nevertheless, that first cry—"Yes, yes—why not?"—had served to wake the wish to have this question answered. For it was suddenly evident to everyone present that something was, indeed, at fault. Those who had known Griffith longest must have been the most bewildered. How could a man whose earliest, most obscure, most anonymous work in films had been so clearly marked with meaning and artistic courage, who had sent out from the Biograph Studio to the nation's nickelodeons month after month films that were amazing fresh strides forward in film expressiveness, who broke down all commercial and cultural barriers around the young medium with an overwhelming first big film, who had manufactured most of the star-pillars that held up the industrial structure, whose most casual film seemed to embody the highest ideals circulating in American films—how could such a man have been allowed to sit for years in the lobby of the Hollywood-Knickerbocker Hotel, talking of past and future dreams to anyone who would listen, while seven of the most splendid studios of the world—all within bus distance—remained closed to him? Nor can we say that *Life's* deadly tribute to the dead master provides any full explanation: "But somehow Griffith, the marvelous innovator, could not keep up with the medium he had created. As America grew more sophisticated his story-sense grew to seem old-fashioned. . . ." This may flatter those Hollywoodites who consider themselves both more sophisticated and more time-repellent; but can we find, among the honorary bearers of Griffith's pall, any who could make such a claim? What is there in Cecil DeMille's *Unconquered* of 1947 that wouldn't blush when compared with Griffith's *America* of 1924? Nor can pallbearers John Ford or Raoul Walsh, not to mention Louis B. Mayer or Jesse Lasky, all of whom are still functioning, in their way, prove their mentalities and "story-sense" more sophisticated!

No, the answer to this question is not to be found in the shifting film worlds of taste and commerce, but in something within the man. What equipment did he bring to films in 1908 when he offered himself as employee, actor, writer, and finally director-controlling artist? The one art in which he had had a varied and excitingly uncertain experience was the theater—and no theatrical period has been more colorful or less substantial than the American theater that sprawled over the turning century. From ten years of acting, young Griffith brought to films a surer sense of theatricality than they had known, and in films he found himself among people who knew less and had experienced less than he. His spare-time love and dream was literature: plays, verse, stories, all were in constant process, some even reached the stage or print. From this love he brought enthusiasm and vague notions of art to his film work; and from his Biograph films to his last effort, *The Struggle* [1931], one sees this literary luggage as mixed—offering amplitudes of thematic ambition unsupported by real knowledge of the nature of literature, or of any art.

As it was a new untried art he had wandered into, this may appear to have been no disadvantage. But it now seems clear that he might well have wandered out again as easily if a concreteness in some part of this field had not been found outside himself. His enthusiasm and energy won him the sixteen-year artistic partnership of G. W. "Billy" Bitzer, a man who knew his job so well that he was always able to teach Griffith as much as he learned from that original artist. The cameraman handed the director unlimited ingenuity and good sense, and the combination of their two minds and talents was unbeatable. The whole undiscovered medium of film lay before them, and they were greedy to explore it. The hundreds of films they made together at Biograph could not all be masterpieces; but no one else can be said to have enlarged the scope of any art as swiftly as did Griffith and Bitzer in those vivid brief reels, and the later two-reelers that they talked the firm into letting them make. Anyone unable to examine these unpolished treasures can see their culminative richness in *The Birth of a Nation*.

This film is a constant anxiety to honest critics: "How can I admit artistic or even technical greatness in a film that has written such a history of injury and misuse?" Evasion of this contradiction usually transfers the laurels and emphasis to the "less harmful" *Intolerance*. Another evasion of this critical hazard is to reject totally the injurious film. This does justice neither to an important film nor to truth, in whose name the rejection is usually made.

This film-goer has learned to look at *The Birth of a Nation* as at two distinct films—and it is the second of these that contains not only the racist melodrama and raw historical distortion of Thomas Dixon's penny-dreadfuls, but also the most dazzling and least useful of Griffith's innovations. The ride of the Klan cleared the road for more than fresh fears and bloodlettings; here was the pattern for the cheapest and most hollow film sensations, the ornament of every film that hoped to stamp out all intellectual stimulus with a brutal physical impact on its audience. Even Veblen's recorded comment on this film accurately reflects its misused skill: "Never before have I seen such concise misinformation." One could suspect that, unconsciously, the dynamics of this part of the film were intended to drive from the spectator's mind those thoughts and questions roused by the film's first half.

For me this first part is self-contained, ending on one of the greatest and most tragically final images of all film-time—the open arms that welcome the returning colonel, stumbling across the pillared porch to his unseen but not unaltered family. This is a film that repays the most minute and repeated examination. In this film (that I think of as "The War" as distinct from the other, "The Klan") the genius and inventive passion of Griffith were at their peak. This is a film that carries forward his Biograph lyrics and dramas and, perhaps more importantly, offers the riches of Griffith's creative experience only to his most deserving director-pupils. For the emotion behind the scenes of war, and the thought they provoke, have made the methods of these scenes useless to the sensation-mongers. They are at once a summing up of two generations' deepest feelings about a civil war, and a revelation of these feelings in images that will ever vitalize that event as much as Brady's photographs,[1] Melville's poems, and Winslow Homer's drawings. But when we look for those film-makers who pursued these courageous filmic thrusts to the spectator's heart and brain, we find few of them in the history of Hollywood; they are the Soviet film-makers, particularly Pudovkin, the most apt pupil of the master. Some of the most witheringly accusing scenes in *The End of St. Petersburg* derive their motive power not only from the expected source of *Intolerance,* but just as much from the battle scenes of "The War."

If any fault is to be found in this half of *The Birth of a Nation,* it is sentiment; but the presence of sentiment, even bathetic (though many passages ascend to genuine pathos), does not seem so serious a matter in comparison with the moral and aesthetic mayhem suffered every week by helpless film audiences. Sentiment can even be a rich and positive source for art, but it makes a risky partner for an unpracticed brain.

---

[1] Before Bitzer's death some years ago he gave Beaumont Newhall details on the actual use of these photographs by Griffith during the shooting of the war-time scenes—indicating a respect for Brady and his group undemonstrated by the makers of later Civil War films.

Anyone who would underestimate the bond between sentiment and craft in Griffith's work need only read this record [2] of a reporter sent to the Mutual Studio on Sunset Boulevard to see what Griffith was doing with *The Clansman*. The scene is the slave-quarters:

> He sits in a chair on a little platform in front and a little to the side of the camera, wearing a tattered straw hat, his cigar and his megaphone in action. A half-dozen Negro boys are "acting" in the foreground. He doesn't scream to them that that will not do. His hand dives into his pocket; it comes forth full of dimes. He tosses a dozen into the group.
>
> "Scramble for 'em!" he calls. "That's it! Laugh and cut up! Now, there's another dime for each of you if you do it again, and do it right. That's it!"
>
> Then his eye travels two hundred feet away, the megaphone comes to his lips:
>
> "Out a little more back there! Hit it up, Bill! You two men near the cabin get to dancing! That's it!"
>
> Back to the foreground again:
>
> "Take the hat off that banjo player—it shades his face. Now—all ready! Dance, there—dance! That's it! You children run right back through the crowd now. You white folks come up to the center! You —in that chair! Put back your head—go to sleep and snore!"

Though ludicrously naïve, this is not the picture of a criminal preparing a crime. This is a sentimental reconstruction of a world that the builder's childhood, his parents and his grandparents had demonstrated to him as the only world worth living in, the only one in which the Griffiths would be happy and secure. The point is not to excuse *The Birth of a Nation*—it is too big an achievement to demand anything less than understanding. It would have been a miracle if the son of Colonel "Roaring Jake" Griffith had reconstructed any more temperate or reasoned or objective picture of the South—or of his own outlook on life and history. And it was a mixture of this sentimental cloud over the past and a bitterness that enveloped his present that dictated his final instructions—to have his body sent away from Hollywood to a Kentucky cemetery.

I know that to some it will sound like quibbling with Dante, but to me *Intolerance*, like *The Birth of a Nation*, seems a towering compound of greatness and cheapness, and, to use Harry Potamkin's phrase on the earlier film, "more grandiose than grand." For the more moved

---

[2] Selwyn A. Stanhope, "The World's Master Picture Producer," in *Photoplay Magazine* (January, 1915).

one is by its bold strokes of original vision, invention, realism, the more intolerant one becomes of the florid theatricality and tinsel that block whole passages. One is forced to conclude that the Griffith genius must have had even greater force than is claimed for it by the idolaters in order to have accomplished so much under the burden of the tawdriest theater traditions.

A simple division of *Intolerance* into the worthy and the worthless is impossible. One cannot say even that the humanity of its modern story is unscorched by the fireworks of technical sensationalism, nor that the gaudy Babylonian episode is untouched by delicacy and human observation. In the same breath you bless and curse the idea of weaving together these stories that bear so little significant relation to each other. Here, too, one sees a huge jerry-built frame of ideals enclosing a picture that strives with all its author's hampered might to fill that frame. The origin of *Intolerance* in Griffith's wish to answer the unanswerable attacks on *The Birth of a Nation* added plenty of inflated passion to the new film without a balancing amount of substance.

This war between passion and substance went on, with Griffith as both battlefield and victim. His next film, *Hearts of the World*, was a propaganda assignment whose passionate falsity would have finished any lesser man. The films that followed posed the hugest of subjects—uprooted peoples, social crimes, the French Revolution, the American Revolution, postwar Germany, and so on—but his mental equipment grew progressively unwilling to cope with these dimensions. We were given atmospheres and sequences of great beauty (*Broken Blossoms*) and of skillfully extended tension (the climax of *Way Down East*), but the artistic death sounded by the ride of the Klan was irremediable. None of Griffith's frustrating conflicts with the banks and the exhibitors was as bloody as the conflict with his own inadequacies. An instinct for beauty clashed with a desperate wish for "culture," rarely finding an embodiment more substantial than big words—"intolerance" was the biggest and emptiest of these. From *A Corner in Wheat* to *Intolerance*—and, fatally, beyond—the "social" theme was reduced to the "social cliché," employed for effect rather than for any fierce need felt by the maker himself. His poetic genius was twisted as far out of its most productive course as any talent in American history.

Hard, difficult thought was not a part of D. W.'s make-up. If logic and reasoning had been sought by him to give real, rather than artificial weight to his natural lyrical and sensual effects, his film-making would have continued right up to July 23, 1948. In his disciple, Pudovkin, the wish has been almost as one-sided (and on the same side, too), but in his case another social setting provided the demands and the encouragement to offset his dependence on the senses; the result in

Pudovkin's case has not been to maintain the initial high sensual excitement, which fades without sufficient intellectual food, but at least the master-pupil Pudovkin continues to produce what he does best—films. Looking at Pudovkin we can imagine what might have happened to Griffith if transposed (as he nearly was, by Lenin's invitation, in 1919!) to that different society, with its different aims and different demands.

In film history 1948 will always be remembered as a year of loss. No area of world film production has been left unharmed, by anti-freedom committees, by bullying trade-pacts, or by the death of pioneer artists, such as [Urban] Gad in Denmark and [Jacques] Feyder in France. Six months before Griffith's death, we lost an artist who, in learning from Griffith, lifted the lessons taught so unconsciously to a supreme consciousness, of idea and art. When we mourn Griffith, let us too count up our debt to Sergei Eisenstein. The anti-intellectualism of the one and the super-intellectuality of the other together formed the backbone of film art in its first fifty years of life. From neither have we learned all he could teach us; our learning will be the most handsome memorial we can erect to them.

The Films of D. W. Griffith

Except for the first entry, the following list indicates only Griffith's longer, feature films. A listing of his 494 one- and two-reel Biograph pictures, made during the period 1908–14, is to be found in Iris Barry and Eileen Bowser, *D. W. Griffith: American Film Master* (New York: The Museum of Modern Art, 1965), pp. 40–43. A more elaborate, annotated listing of the Biograph films of Griffith appears in Robert M. Henderson, *D. W. Griffith: The Years at Biograph* (New York: Farrar, Straus and Giroux, 1970), pp. 193–215, supplemented by indexes to the players in those films and the authors and sources of many of the film stories. The main text of Henderson's book provides summaries of many of the Biograph films and indicates technical advances where they occur. Other summaries of some of the Biograph films appear in Kemp R. Niver, *Motion Pictures from The Library of Congress Paper Print Collection: 1894–1912* (Berkeley and Los Angeles: University of California Press, 1967).

In the list that follows, the title of the film is given, and then: (1) Name of Producing Company; (2) Name of Cameraman. Cast lists and other details are available in Iris Barry and Eileen Bowser, see above.

1908   *The Adventures of Dollie*; released July 14. (1) the Biograph Company; (2) Arthur Marvin. This was the first film Griffith directed. *1 reel.*

1914   *Judith of Bethulia.* (1) the Biograph Company; (2) G. W. "Billy" Bitzer. DWG's last film for the Biograph Company. *4 reels.*

         The Battle of the Sexes. (1) the Mutual Film Corporation; (2) Bitzer.

         The Escape. (1) the Mutual Film Corporation; (2) Bitzer.

         Home, Sweet Home. (1) the Mutual Film Corporation; (2) Bitzer.

         The Avenging Conscience. (1) the Mutual Film Corporation; (2) Bitzer.

1915 *The Birth of a Nation.* (1) Epoch Producing Corporation; (2) Bitzer.

1916 *Intolerance.* (1) Wark Producing Corporation; (2) Bitzer.

1918 *Hearts of the World.* (1) Artcraft Pictures; (2) Bitzer.

   The Great Love. (1) Artcraft Pictures; (2) Bitzer.

   The Greatest Thing in Life. (1) Artcraft Pictures (2)?

1919 *A Romance of Happy Valley.* (1) Artcraft Pictures (2)?

   The Girl Who Stayed at Home. (1) Artcraft Pictures (2)?

   True Heart Susie. (1) Artcraft Pictures (2)?

   Scarlet Days. (1) Artcraft Pictures (2)?

   Broken Blossoms. (1) Independently produced by DWG and later distributed by United Artists; (2) Bitzer.

   The Greatest Question. (1) First National Pictures; (2) Bitzer.

1920 *The Idol Dancer.* (1) First National Pictures; (2) Bitzer.

   The Love Flower. (1) First National Pictures; (2) Bitzer.

   Way Down East. (1) United Artists; (2) Bitzer and Hendrick Sartov.

1921 *Dream Street.* (1) United Artists; (2)?

   Orphans of the Storm. (1) United Artists; (2) Hendrick Sartov.

1922 *One Exciting Night.* (1) United Artists; (2) Hendrick Sartov.

1923 *The White Rose.* (1) United Artists; (2) Bitzer.

1924 *America.* (1) United Artists; (2) Bitzer.

   Isn't Life Wonderful. (1) United Artists; (2) Hendrick Sartov and Hal Sintzenich.

1925 *Sally of the Sawdust.* (1) Paramount Pictures; (2) Harry Fischbeck and Hal Sintzenich.

1926 *That Royle Girl.* (1) Paramount Pictures; (2) Harry Fischbeck and Hal Sintzenich.

   The Sorrows of Satan. (1) Paramount Pictures; (2) Harry Fischbeck.

1928 *Drums of Love.* (1) Art Cinema Corporation/United Artists; (2) Bitzer, Karl Struss, and Harry Jackson.

   The Battle of the Sexes. (1) Art Cinema Corporation/United Artists; (2) Bitzer and Karl Struss.

1929 *Lady of the Pavements.* (1) Cinema Corporation/United Artists; (2) Karl Struss with assistance from Bitzer.

1930   *Abraham Lincoln.* (1) Art Cinema Corporation/United
            Artists; (2) Karl Struss.

1931   *The Struggle.* (1) D. W. Griffith, Inc.; (2) Joseph Rutten-
            berg.

The largest rental collection of Griffith films is that of The Museum
of Modern Art, Department of Film, 11 West 53 Street, New York,
N. Y. 10019. Consult MOMA film library catalog for specific titles. 8-
mm. and Super-8 prints of *America, Broken Blossoms, The Fall of
Babylon, Hearts of the World, Intolerance, Judith of Bethulia, Orphans of the Storm,* and *Way Down East* may be purchased from Blackhawk Films, The Eastin-Phelan Corporation, Davenport, Iowa 52808.
Blackhawk also sells prints of many of Griffith's one- and two-reel Biograph pictures in 8-mm. Super-8 and 16-mm. See further current Blackhawk *Bulletin* for full details and prices. Prints of other Biograph pictures by Griffith, in 16-mm. may be purchased from Historical Films,
Box 46505, Hollywood, California 90046.

Selected Bibliography

1. ARTICLES AND INTERVIEWS BY GRIFFITH—
   IN CHRONOLOGICAL ORDER

"Replies to Two Questions." In Robert Grau, *The Theatre of Science.* New York: Broadway Publishing Co., 1914, pp. 85–87. Text of letter by DWG.

"D. W. Griffith, Producer of the World's Biggest Picture." *New York American,* February 28, 1915, City Life and Dramatic Section, p. 9. Interview conducted in connection with the New York premiere of *The Birth of a Nation.*

"Five Dollar 'Movies' Prophesied." *The Editor,* April 24, 1915, pp. 407–10. Article by DWG.

Gordon, Henry Stephen. "The Story of David Wark Griffith." *Photoplay,* X (June, 1916), 28–37, 162–64; (July, 1916), 122–32; (August, 1916), 78–88; (September, 1916), 146–48; (October, 1916), 86–94; (November, 1916), 27–40. Biography based extensively on interviews with DWG; details of his work on *The Birth of a Nation* and *Intolerance.*

The Rise and Fall of Free Speech in America. Los Angeles: Published by the author, 1916. 45-page pamphlet by DWG, provoked by protests against *The Birth of a Nation.*

"Pictures vs. One-Night Stands." *Independent* (December 11, 1916), pp. 447–48. Article by DWG.

"What I Demand of Movie Stars." *Moving Picture Classic* (February, 1917), pp. 40–41, 68. Article by DWG.

B., O. M. "The Film World's Greatest Achievement." *Pictures and the Picturegoer* (London): April 28, 1917). Interview with DWG during his filming of *Intolerance.* He indicates that some themes for the film were developed out of his Biograph two-reeler, *The Reformers,* of *The Lost Art of Minding One's Business* (1913); he also states that he works without scripts: "I carry the whole scheme and the smallest detail of production in my mind." He indicates further that he prefers spending a week coaching an inexperienced girl who *looks* the part to ten minutes working with an experienced actress: ". . . looking the part is half the battle. . . ."

"Griffith Returns to America." *Pictures and the Picturegoer* (London: November 24, 1917), p. 559. Interview.

Carr, Harry C. "Griffith, Maker of Battle Scenes, Sees Real War." *Photoplay* (March, 1918), pp. 23–28. Interview.

————. "How Griffith Picks His Leading Women." *Photoplay* (December, 1918), pp. 24–25. Interview.

"Life and the Photodrama." *Motion Picture Classic* (December, 1918), pp. 16–17, 70. Article by DWG.

"Motion Pictures: The Miracle of Modern Photography." *The Mentor* (July 1, 1921), pp. 3–12. Article by DWG, containing a brief survey of cinema prehistory.

"Youth, the Spirit of the Movies." *Illustrated World* (October, 1921), pp. 194–96. Article by DWG.

"Are Motion Pictures Destructive of Good Taste?" *Arts and Decoration* (September, 1923), pp. 12–13, 79. Article by DWG.

"The Real Truth About Breaking Into the Movies." *Woman's Home Companion* (February, 1924), pp. 16, 138. Article by DWG. Indicates that "faithful work as an extra" is the only way for a beginning actor to break into the movies, and warns would-be movie stars that "it is impossible to emphasize too much the essential uncertainty of the whole business. . . . Success for the amateur picture player is not impossible. It is merely improbable."

"How Do You Like the Show?" *Collier's* (April 24, 1924), pp. 8–9. Article by DWG.

"The Movies 100 Years From Now." *Collier's* (May 3, 1924), pp. 7, 28. Article by DWG. The article is reprinted in Harry M. Geduld, ed., *Film-Makers on Film-Making* (Bloomington, Ind.: Indiana University Press, 1967), pp. 49–55.

"Don't Blame the Movies!" *Motion Picture Magazine* (July, 1926), pp. 33, 82. Article by DWG.

Tully, Jim. "David Wark Griffith." *Vanity Fair* (November, 1926), pp. 80, 110. Interview.

"Pace in the Movies," Liberty (November 13, 1926), pp. 19, 21. Article by DWG. Argues that "the touchstone of a picture's appeal is pace; pace is the secret of the director's art."

"The Greatest Theatrical Force." *Moving Picture World* (March 26, 1927), p. 408. Article by DWG.

"The Motion Picture Today and Tomorrow." *Theatre* (October, 1927), pp. 21, 58. Article by DWG.

"Tomorrow's Motion Picture." *The Picturegoer* (London: June, 1928), p. 11. Article by DWG. Claims that "motion pictures are really a *new* form of literary and artistic expression. This fact was recognized in the beginning . . . later on, it seemed to be lost sight of entirely . . . Must it [the screen] be the step-child of literature, forever wearing remodelled garments . . . ?"

Letter by DWG. In *Register of the Kentucky State Historical Society,* XXVI, no. 76 (1928), pp. 92–93. Brief reminiscences of his boyhood in Kentucky ("In memory LaGrange and Oldham County seem to me naturally the fairest of all lands") and of his father. Claims that he is proudest of all at being "the son of Col. Jacob Griffith, a son of the Confederacy and of the State of Kentucky. . . ."

"What is Beauty in Motion Pictures?" *Liberty* (October 19, 1929), pp. 28–29. Article by DWG. States that beauty in the motion picture "is the pleasing presentation of the thing for which people are yearning."

"An Old-Timer Advises Hollywood." *Liberty* (June 17, 1939), p. 18. Article by DWG.

2. Secondary Sources: Books

Aitken, Roy E., and Al P. Nelson. *The "Birth of a Nation" Story.* Middleburg, Va.; A Denlinger Book, 1965. 95-page reminiscence by one of the film's producers.

Arvidson, Linda. *See* Griffith, Linda Arvidson.

Barry, Iris. *D. W. Griffith: American Film Master.* New York: The Museum of Modern Art, 1940. 40 pages.

Barry, Iris and Eileen Bowser. *D. W. Griffith: American Film Master.* New York: The Museum of Modern Art, 1965. 88-page revized and enlarged edition of Iris Barry's earlier work. Provides fundamental factual material on Griffith and his films. Check-list of the Biograph films and credits and cast-lists of all the later work of DWG.

Boston Branch of the National Association for the Advancement of Colored People. *Fighting a Vicious Film: Protest Against "The Birth of a Nation."* Boston, Mass., Boston Branch of the NAACP, 1915. 47-page pamphlet. Miscellany of protest and hostile criticism of the film by such commentators as Francis Hackett, Oswald Garrison Villard, and Booker T. Washington.

Brownlow, Kevin. *The Parade's Gone By.* New York: Alfred A. Knopf, 1968. 577 pp. Wealth of miscellaneous material on DWG, including reminiscences by Joseph Henabery and Mary Pickford, and many excellent stills.

Croy, Homer. *Star Maker: The Story of D. W. Griffith.* Introduction by Mary Pickford. New York: Duell, Sloan & Pearce, 1959. 210 pages. Inaccurate, unreliable, and quite unworthy biography of DWG.

Gish, Lillian with Ann Pinchot. *The Movies, Mr. Griffith, and Me.* Englewood Cliffs, N.J.; Prentice-Hall, Inc., 1969. 388-page memoir of DWG and recollections of his films in the making—by his leading actress.

Goodman, Ezra. *The Fifty Year Decline and Fall of Hollywood.* New York: Macfadden, Bartell, 1957. 312 pages. The first chapter deals with DWG's closing years.

Griffith, Linda Arvidson (Mrs. D. W. Griffith). *When the Movies Were Young.* New York: E. P. Dutton Co., 1925. 227 pages. Memoir of DWG's life and work through *The Birth of a Nation.* Primary source material.

Hastings, Charles Edward and Herman Holland. *A Biography of David Wark Griffith.* New York: D. W. Griffith Service, n.d., but presumably prior to 1915. Contains interesting comments by DWG on the need for extending motion pictures to a length of eight to twelve reels: ". . . the thing I am working for is an evening's entertainment made up of one complete picture." He insists that special music is needed for films: "Original scores are very interesting to me, personally. I like to take a deep interest in the music intended for use in connection with my pictures."

Henderson, Robert M. *D. W. Griffith: The Years at Biograph.* New York: Farrar, Straus and Giroux, 1970. 250 pages. Well-researched study of DWG's film-work prior to *The Birth of a Nation.* Contains annotated list of DWG's Biograph films and useful bibliography that includes a section on unpublished material—including papers in the Griffith archive at the Museum of Modern Art.

Huff, Theodore. *A Shot Analysis of D. W. Griffith's "The Birth of a Nation."* New York: The Museum of Modern Art, 1961. 62 pages.
———. *"Intolerance": The Film by David Wark Griffith: Shot-by-Shot Analysis.* New York: The Museum of Modern Art, 1966. 155 pages.

Jacobs, Lewis. *The Rise of the American Film.* New York: Harcourt, Brace and Co., 1939. 585 pages. Republished in New York by Teachers College Press, 1967, with additional material concerning experimental cinema in America, 1921–1947. Chapters VII, XI, and XIX are devoted to DWG. Chapter XIX, "The Decline of D. W. Griffith," has occasioned much controversy among critics who disagree with Mr. Jacobs' view that DWG's later films are "the work of a man who was no longer influencing movies but being influenced by them."

Kerr, Judge Charles [ed.] *History of Kentucky.* Chicago and New York: Connelly & Coulter, 1922. See vol. V, 638–40 for factual summaries of the lives of DWG and his father.

Lindsay, Vachel. *The Art of the Moving Picture.* New York: Macmillan, 1915. 289 pages. Republished in New York by Liveright, 1970, with an introduction by Stanley Kauffman. The major critical and aesthetic film study of its period—still significant reading; contains much important commentary on the work of DWG.

Long, Robert E. *David Wark Griffith, A Brief Sketch of His Career.* New York: The Museum of Modern Art, 1946. 38 pages.

Loos, Anita. *A Girl Like I.* New York: The Viking Press, 1966. 275 pages. Contains recollections by DWG by one of his most talented screenwriters.

Macgowan, Kenneth. *Behind the Screen: The History and Techniques of the Motion Picture.* New York: Delacorte Press, 1965. 528 pages. Much material on DWG in Chapters 9 through 12. Uneven and sometimes unreliable.

Macdonald, Dwight. *On Movies.* Englewood Cliffs, N.J.: Prentice-Hall, Inc., 1969. See "D. W. Griffith, Or Genius American Style," pp. 70–73. Macdonald argues that Griffith's genius "seems to be purely instinctive" and that he was "a typically American product. He is to the cinema what Edison is to science: a practical genius who can make things work but who is not interested in theory, i.e., the general laws that govern his achievements." Macdonald describes his experience of spending an evening with DWG during the thirties: "he looked and behaved like an old-style ham actor. . . . He was quite drunk. . . . We couldn't get him talking on the magnificent technique [of *Intolerance*]. . . . Griffith . . . to this day remains, except for Eisenstein, the most creative user of the two basic elements in cinematic technique, montage and the close-up; but when he thought, he was a child. . . ."

O'Dell, Paul. *Griffith and the Rise of Hollywood.* Announced as a forthcoming publication at the time this book was being prepared for the press.

Petersen, Ruth C., and L. L. Thurstone. *Motion Pictures and the Social Attitudes of Children.* New York: The Macmillan Company, 1933. 75 pages. One of the volumes in the Payne Fund Studies. Pages 35–38, 60–61 contain a report on a survey carried out among 434 students at a school in Crystal Lake, Illinois, a town in which there were no blacks. Petersen and Thurstone investigated the attitude of the children towards blacks before and after the showing of *The Birth of a Nation*, and also five months after the movie had been screened. Their first conclusion, from the inquiries made soon after the film had been shown, was that the film "had the effect of making the children less favorable to the Negro"; their conclusion months later, after further inquiry, was that the effect of the film "on the children's attitude toward the Negro was still definitely present eight months after the film was shown."

Pickford, Mary. *Sunshine and Shadow*. New York: Doubleday, 1955. 382 pages. Reminiscences of DWG by one of his most famous stars.

Pratt, George C. *Spellbound in Darkness*. Rochester, New York: The University of Rochester School of Liberal & Applied Studies, 1966. In two volumes: volume I, pp. 1–197; volume II, pp. 201–452. Rich collection of reviews and commentaries on film, culled from journals and newspapers of the silent era. Chapters 4, 5, 6, 11, and 15 focus on DWG.

Ramsaye, Terry. *A Million and One Nights*. New York: Simon & Schuster, 1926. 868 pages. Chapters 44, 50, 53, 60, 63, and 76 contain most of Ramsaye's material on DWG, much of which has been augmented and corrected by more recent works.

Robinson, David. *Hollywood in the Twenties*. London & New York: A. Zwemmer & A. S. Barnes, 1968. 176 pages. Contains a brief survey of the later work of DWG.

Vardac, A. Nicolas. *Stage to Screen: Theatrical Method from Garrick to Griffith*. Cambridge, Mass.: Harvard University Press, 1949. 283 pages. Republished in New York and London by Benjamin Blom, 1968. Deals with ways in which the motion picture took over traditions of melodrama. Chapters IX through XI discuss the techniques of DWG and their relation to theatrical methods.

Wagenknecht, Edward. *The Movies in the Age of Innocence*. Norman, Oklahoma: University of Oklahoma Press, 1962. 280 pages. Valuable commentary on American silent cinema. One chapter is devoted to DWG; contains a useful bibliographical note on pp. 80–84.

SECONDARY SOURCES: ARTICLES AND PERIODICALS

Arvidson, Linda. *See* Griffith, Linda Arvidson.

Brakhage, Stan. "David Wark Griffith," *Caterpillar* #13 (October 1970), 103–121. Heretical but provocative commentary by a notable avant-garde film-maker.

Codd, E. "The War Film and D. W. Griffith." *Pictures and Picturegoer* (London: July 13, 1918), pp. 54, 56. Critique of *Hearts of the World* in the context of DWG's earlier films.

Cozarinsky, Edgardo. "Permanencia de David Wark Griffith." *Film Ideal*, no. 172 (July 15, 1965), pp. 471–80. In Spanish. Interesting study of DWG's influences on later film-makers.

Crisp, Donald. "David W. Griffith: The Man and His Methods." *The Picturegoer* (London: January, 1921), pp. 14–15. DWG at work as described by one of his leading actors. Crisp maintains that DWG's greatness as a director was due to his "skill in handling the human element" in the studio, and to his "unique knowledge of human nature in general."

Dickinson, Thorold. "Griffith and the Development of the Silent Film." *Sight and Sound* (October–December, 1951), pp. 84ff.

Dorris, George E. "Griffith in Retrospect." In W. R. Robinson, *Man and the Movies*. Baltimore, Md.: Penguin Books, 1967, pp. 153–60. Sympathetic survey of DWG's work based on the 1965 Griffith retrospective programs at The Museum of Modern Art.

Eisenstein, Sergei. "Dickens, Griffith, and the Film Today." In the same author's *Film Form*. London: Dennis Dobson, 1951, pp. 195–255. A major critical and analytical study of Griffith and the sources of his techniques; obligatory reading for any serious student of DWG and Eisenstein.

Everson, William K. "Griffith and Realism: Apropos *The Birth of a Nation* (1915)." *Cinemages,* no. 5 (1955), pp. 14–17. Defends the film from DWG's standpoint as depicting an accurate and impartial account of the South's role in the Civil War, thus, in DWG's words, "representing in art . . . things as they actually are." Important commentary and analysis.

———. "The Films of D. W. Griffith 1907–1934." *Screen Facts* (May–June, 1963), pp. 1–27. "This article is not intended so much as a critical survey of Griffith's films as a complete and up-to-date listing of them. . . ."

Film Culture: Special Griffith issue. See Stern, Seymour. "Griffith: 1— *The Birth of a Nation.*"

Goodman, Paul. "Film Chronicle: Griffith and the Technical Innovations." *Partisan Review* (May–June, 1941), pp. 237–40.

Griffith, Linda Arvidson (Mrs. D. W. Griffith). "Early Struggles of Motion Picture Stars." In *Film Flashes,* New York: Leslie Judge Company, 1916, pp. 5ff.

Harrison, Louis Reeves. "David W. Griffith: the Art Director and His Work." *Moving Picture World* (November 22, 1913), pp. 847–48.

Manuel, Jacques. "D. W. G. Panorama de l'Oeuvre de Griffith: 1914–1931." *La Revue du Cinéma* (Paris: November, 1946), pp. 14–36. Uneven and sometimes inaccurate survey of DWG's mature work.

Moving Picture World, The. Consult issues from 1908 onwards for reviews and comments on the work of DWG.

Mullett, Mary B. "Greatest Moving Picture Producer in the World." *American Magazine* (April, 1921), pp. 32–34, 144, 146, 148.

New York Dramatic Mirror, The. Consult issues from 1908 onwards for comments on Griffith and his work.

New York Times, The. Numerous reviews of Griffith's films. See Volume I of *The New York Times Film Reviews.* New York: The New York Times & Arno Press, 1970.

Noble, Peter. "A Note on an Idol." *Sight and Sound* (Autumn, 1946), p. 81. Iconoclastic. See the replies in the same journal, Spring, 1947, p. 32.

Sterling, Philip. "Billy Bitzer, Ace Cameraman," *New Theatre,* April 1937, pp. 29–30, 46. Study of the work and later career of DWG's cameraman on many of his films. Observes: "if a medal is ever stamped with the face of David Wark Griffith, its obverse side will have to bear the likeness of Billy Bitzer. . . . The collective nature of film art made it inevitable that he [Griffith] should share his efforts and his glory with others, and most of all with Billy Bitzer."

Stern, Seymour. "An Index to the Creative Work of D. W. Griffith." *Index Series,* British Film Institute, nos. 2, 4, 7, 8, 10 (April, 1944).

———. "The Griffith Controversy." *Sight and Sound* (Spring, 1948), pp. 49–50. Long letter.

———. "The Cold War against David Wark Griffith." *Films in Review* (February, 1956), pp. 49–59. Vigorous defence of DWG against what Stern considers to be a Communist conspiracy to destroy the director's reputation.

———. "Biographical Hogwash." *Films in Review* (May, 1959), pp. 284–96. First part of a two-part review-analysis of Homer Croy's book on DWG, exposing the numerous inaccuracies and shortcomings of that work.

———. "Biographical Hogwash: Part 2." *Films in Review* (June–July, 1959), pp. 336–43. Part two of Stern's review of Homer Croy's book on DWG. Letters critical of Stern's analysis and facts appear in the same journal, issue for September 1959, pp. 441ff.

———. "Griffith: 1—*The Birth of a Nation.*" *Film Culture* no. 36. Spring–Summer, 1965), 214 pages. The entire issue is devoted to Stern's treatise on *The Birth of a Nation.* Mixture of useful factual material and protracted observations on Stern's belief that a Communist conspiracy has been assailing DWG's reputation. Many excellent stills from the film.

Turner, W. B. "The Greatness of Griffith." *Pictures and Picturegoer* (London: August, 1925), p. 46. Brief discussion of DWG's work and reputation. "Griffith so evidently wants to preach Humanity rather than depict History and to practice Simplicity in lieu of Subtlety. . . ."

Vincent, Carl. "Parabola storica di David Wark Griffith." *Bianco e Nero* (December, 1948), pp. 48–58. In Italian. Critical survey of the work of DWG.

Secondary Sources: Unpublished Commentary

Hutchins, Charles L. *A Critical Evaluation of the Controversies Engendered by D. W. Griffith's "The Birth of a Nation."* M.A. dissertation, University of Iowa, 1961.

Index